e	o
げ	ご
ぜ	ぞ
で	ど

e	o
べ	ぼ
ぺ	ぽ

c\v	a	u	o
ky	きゃ	きゅ	きょ
sh	しゃ	しゅ	しょ
ch	ちゃ	ちゅ	ちょ
ny	にゃ	にゅ	にょ
hy	ひゃ	ひゅ	ひょ

c\v	a	u	o
my	みゃ	みゅ	みょ

c\v	a	u	o
ry	りゃ	りゅ	りょ

c\v	a	u	o
gy	ぎゃ	ぎゅ	ぎょ
jy	じゃ	じゅ	じょ
dy	ぢゃ	ぢゅ	ぢょ

c\v	a	u	o
by	びゃ	びゅ	びょ
py	ぴゃ	ぴゅ	ぴょ

e	o
ゲ	ゴ
ゼ	ゾ
デ	ド

e	o
ベ	ボ
ペ	ポ

c\v	a	u	o
ky	キャ	キュ	キョ
sh	シャ	シュ	ショ
ch	チャ	チュ	チョ
ny	ニャ	ニュ	ニョ
hy	ヒャ	ヒュ	ヒョ

c\v	a	u	o
my	ミャ	ミュ	ミョ

c\v	a	u	o
ry	リャ	リュ	リョ

c\v	a	u	o
gy	ギャ	ギュ	ギョ
jy	ジャ	ジュ	ジョ
dy	ヂャ	ヂュ	ヂョ

c\v	a	u	o
by	ビャ	ビュ	ビョ
py	ピャ	ピュ	ピョ

ti	di
ティ	ディ

fa	fo
ファ	フォ

Japanese for Young People II

Student Book

JAPANESE FOR YOUNG PEOPLE

 **Student Book**

Association for Japanese-Language Teaching

Kodansha International
Tokyo • New York • London

The Authors: The Association for Japanese-Language Teaching (AJALT) was recognized as a nonprofit organization by the Ministry of Education in 1977. It was established to meet the practical needs of people who are not necessarily specialists on Japan but who wish to communicate effectively in Japanese. In 1992 the Association was awarded the Japan Foundation Special Prize.

The Association maintains a web site on the Internet at www. ajalt.org and can be contacted over the Internet via info @ajalt.org by teachers and students who have questions about this textbook or any of the Association's other publications.

All illustrations by Hidemi Makino.

Distributed in the United States by Kodansha America, Inc., 575 Lexington Avenue, New York, New York 10022, and in the United Kingdom and continental Europe by Kodansha Europe Ltd., Tavern Quay, Rope Street, London SE16 7TX.

Published by Kodansha International Ltd., 17-14 Otowa 1-chome, Bunkyo-ku, Tokyo 112-8652, and Kodansha America, Inc.

First Edition, 1999
03 04 05 06 07 08 09 10   10 9 8 7 6 5 4 3 2

www.thejapanpage.com

CONTENTS

Lesson 16 — HERE, THERE, AND OVER THERE　たいいくかんは　どこですか。

Functions	Situations	Structures, Expressions, & Vocabulary Sets
• Talking about location • Showing hesitation • Saying thank you casually	school railroad station in town	VERBS 　あります　います COUNTERS 「〜かい」 page 5 SUMMARY TABLE Complete こーそーあーど page 8 「あのう〜」 「どうも」

Lesson 17 — DESCRIBING A PHOTOGRAPH　食どうに　おかあさんが　います。

Functions	Situations	Structures, Expressions, & Vocabulary Sets
• Talking about existence	home department store	LOCATION MARKERS （上　下　中　前　うしろ　となり） VOCABULARY BUILDER 1: Animals page 13

Lesson 18 — EXPLAINING PLACES AND LOCATION　でんわは　スーパーの　前に　あります。

Functions	Situations	Structures, Expressions, & Vocabulary Sets
• Talking about location and existence • Comparison • Showing surprise	in town home school	LOCATION MARKERS （ちかく　みぎ　ひだり） COUNTERS 「〜さつ」 CONNECTING TWO SENTENCES 　「……が、……」 SUMMARY TABLE あります／います page 27

Lesson 19 — SCHOOL LIFE　学校は　たのしいです。

Functions	Situations	Structures, Expressions, & Vocabulary Sets
• States • Expressing opinions • Starting a conversation	school home	「すみませんが、〜について　おしえてください」

Lesson 20 — A JAPANESE FESTIVAL　おまつりは　たのしかったです。

Functions	Situations	Structures, Expressions, & Vocabulary Sets
• Expressing feelings, thoughts, and impressions	school	ADVERBS OF DEGREE SUMMARY TABLE Adjectives page 52 「それは　よかったですね／ざんねんでしたね」

Lesson **21**	A TELEPHONE CALL 友だちに でんわを します。	
Functions	**Situations**	**Structures, Expressions, & Vocabulary Sets**
TELEPHONING •Starting a conversation •Saying goodbye •Saying sorry	school home	VERBS (verbs that take direct/indirect objects) かきます 聞きます おしえます あります でんわを します 「もしもし」 「しつれいします／しつれいしました」 SUMMARY TABLE Family page 63

Lesson **22**	GIVING AND RECEIVING 友だちに ぼうしを もらいました。	
Functions	**Situations**	**Structures, Expressions, & Vocabulary Sets**
GIVING AND RECEIVING	school	VERBS (verbs that take direct/indirect objects) あげます もらいます

Lesson **23**	OWNERSHIP 木村さんは けいたいでんわが あります。	
Functions	**Situations**	**Structures, Expressions, & Vocabulary Sets**
•Talking about possession •Asking about friends and siblings •Explaining about friends and siblings	home after school	VERB あります COUNTERS 「〜だい」 page 83

Lesson **24**	EVENTS 学校で サッカーの しあいが あります。	
Functions	**Situations**	**Structures, Expressions, & Vocabulary Sets**
•Asking and telling about specific events •Asking what something is	school restaurant	VERB あります 「〜って 何ですか」

Lesson **25**	AN INVITATION みんなで おはなみを しませんか。	
Functions	**Situations**	**Structures, Expressions, & Vocabulary Sets**
INVITATIONS •Making an invitation •Accepting / declining an invitation	home school	「すみませんが、ちょっと……。」 「〜は ちょっと……。」

Lesson **26**	ABILITY AND POSSIBILITY この かんじが 分かりません。	
Functions	**Situations**	**Structures, Expressions, & Vocabulary Sets**
•Ability, possibility, and comprehension •Starting a conversation •Saying thank you for something that has already been done	school home	VERBS (verbs that take 「は」and 「が」) できます わかります 「ちょっと いいですか」 「きのうは ありがとうございました」

Lesson **27**	EXPRESSING PREFERENCES から手と じゅうどうと どちらが 好きですか。	
Functions	**Situations**	**Structures, Expressions, & Vocabulary Sets**
•Talking about skills and preferences •Making comparisons	school home store	ADJECTIVES (adjectives that take 「は」と 「が」) 好き（な） じょうず（な） VOCABULARY BUILDER 2: Colors page 133 VOCABULARY BUILDER 3: Vegetables page 136 VOCABULARY BUILDER 4: Fruits page 136 VOCABULARY BUILDER 5: Sport page 136 VOCABULARY BUILDER 6: Musical Instruments page 136

Lesson **28**	SICKNESS のども いたいですか。	
Functions	**Situations**	**Structures, Expressions, & Vocabulary Sets**
•Choosing by comparison •Explaining about where it hurts	hospital school restaurant	ADJECTIVES (adjectives that take 「は」and 「が」) いい いたい VOCABULARY BUILDER 7: The Body page 145

Lesson **29**	TRANSPORTATION まいあさ 八ばんの バスに のります。	
Functions	**Situations**	**Structures, Expressions, & Vocabulary Sets**
•Describing how one gets to a specific destination such as school •Talking about periods of time	school railroad station post office	VERBS のります おります つきます 出ます かかります NOUNS Periods of Time

Lesson **30**	MY FIRST SPEECH まず かぞくに ついて はなします。	
Functions	**Situations**	**Structures, Expressions, & Vocabulary Sets**
MAKING A SPEECH •Talking about oneself, one's family and hometown in a logical structure	public meeting place	ORDINAL CONNECTIVES 「まず」「つぎに」「さいごに」 VOCABULARY BUILDER 8: Occupations page 165

Grammar Review ———————————————————————— page 167

Series Guide to
JAPANESE FOR YOUNG PEOPLE

JAPANESE FOR YOUNG PEOPLE is a new three-level series (with an optional starter level for elementary students) designed primarily for junior high and high school curricula encouraging systematic Japanese-language acquisition through an enjoyable but structured learning process.

Starter Level

Level 1

Japanese for Young People I: Student Book

This first main text in the series introduces basic structures.

Japanese for Young People I: Kana Workbook

A workbook to practice reading and writing the hiragana and katakana native scripts with crossword puzzles, wordsearches and other games that will encourage enjoyable and effective language acquisition.

Level 2

Japanese for Young People II: Student Book

The second main text in the series introduces the conjugation of adjectives and some basic kanji.

Japanese for Young People II: Kanji Workbook

A workbook to practice reading and writing the 70 Chinese characters introduced in the STUDENT BOOK.

Level 3

Japanese for Young People III: Student Book

The third main text in the series introduces verb conjugation and some functional expressions for making requests and asking permission.

Japanese for Young People III: Kanji Workbook

A workbook to practice reading and writing the 80 Chinese characters introduced in the STUDENT BOOK.

Japanese for Young People: Sound & Rhythm

Based on Total Physical Response, this optional level recommended for use by elementary students, encourages pupils to develop essential aural skills by simply listening and following the instructions on the tape. Facilitates smooth progression to Level 1 through familiarization with basic Japanese sounds and words.

Japanese for Young People: Sound & Rhythm Cassette Tapes

Tapes provide essential aural practice through professional recordings from the text.

Japanese for Young People I: Cassette Tapes

Essential aural practice of natural spoken Japanese is facilitated by recordings of marked sections from the STUDENT BOOK. and KANA WORKBOOK.

Japanese for Young People I: Teacher's Book

A step-by-step guide in English for instructors of Japanese with suggested games and activities.

Japanese for Young People II: Cassette Tapes

Essential aural practice of natural spoken Japanese is facilitated by recordings of marked sections from the STUDENT BOOK.

Japanese for Young People II: Teacher's Book

A step-by-step guide in English for instructors of Japanese with suggested games and activities.

Japanese for Young People III: Cassette Tapes

Essential aural practice of natural spoken Japanese is facilitated by recordings of marked sections from the STUDENT BOOK.

Japanese for Young People III: Teacher's Book

A step-by-step guide in English for instructors of Japanese with suggested games and activities.

Learners who complete all levels in this series will have covered one third of the grammatical structures needed for beginner Japanese.

A Note to the Teacher

The Characters

All the characters that appear in JAPANESE FOR YOUNG PEOPLE were specially created and developed with particular emphasis on the kind of situations that target learners are likely to encounter in their daily lives at home and school.

The main protagonist is Mike Bird, a thirteen-year-old American boy who is participating in a student exchange program in Japan. He is living with a representative Japanese family, the Katos, and attends a typical Japanese junior high school.

The Kato family comprises Ken Kato, a boy of the same age as Mike who goes to the same school, his mother and father, and five-year-old sister, Midori. At school Mike makes other friends such as Akira Yamamoto and Sachiko Kimura. He often goes around to Akira's house to play and sometimes meets Akira's mother. Mike's home room teacher is Ms. Keiko Tanaka. A senior from the school Judo club also puts in an appearance.

This collection of protagonists that includes friends of the same age, friends' parents, teachers and seniors reflects the fact that this course has been specially designed to facilitate learners' understanding of how Japanese speech levels depend on interpersonal relationships.

The Plain Style

An important characteristic of the Japanese language is that speech levels change according to whom you are speaking to. Factors such as age, position, or rank most often influence the level of speech in Japanese. This series has adopted a specific policy of familiarizing learners with the different usages of the polite and plain styles from the earliest stages because young people are likely to come across the plain style more often in their linguistic experiences. A dialogue written in the plain style first appears in Lesson 2 of JAPANESE FOR YOUNG PEOPLE I: STUDENT BOOK. In order not to hinder the acquisition of grammatical structures at this introductory stage, however, throughout the series we have decided not to omit any particles simply in the pursuit of reproducing natural Japanese. Similarly, sentence endings are always neutral and no examples of the different endings used by male and female speakers have been included in this book. To start with the plain style is introduced as something that learners should be able to recognize and understand, but in JAPANESE FOR YOUNG PEOPLE III: STUDENT BOOK it is presented as a structure to be learned alongside the plain form of Japanese verbs.

Learners who have not used JAPANESE FOR YOUNG PEOPLE I: STUDENT BOOK are advised to study the Useful Expressions (on pages xxiv–xxvi of the first STUDENT BOOK) before tackling the lessons in this second volume. Also effective for learning common greetings and salutations, this section is an important introduction to the different levels of speech used in Japanese. For each phrase or expression, two appropriate patterns are presented: One that can be used with friends and the other with elders or seniors. More important than learning each greeting, the aim of this section is to make learners aware that Japanese expressions change according to whom one is speaking to.

Script

The native Japanese phonetic scripts, hiragana and katakana, are introduced from the earliest stages of JAPANESE FOR YOUNG PEOPLE I: STUDENT BOOK. Learners are required to have mastered the native hiragana and katakana scripts before starting this book. Learners unfamiliar with kana should complete JAPANESE FOR YOUNG PEOPLE I: KANA WORKBOOK, a fully integrated component of this series, before tackling JAPANESE FOR YOUNG PEOPLE II: STUDENT BOOK.

Learners will be exposed to a total of seventy kanji characters in the fifteen lessons of this book. From the very first lesson of this volume, all words that can be rendered either fully or partially by these seventy kanji are so, but with furigana pronunciation guides printed in small type beneath each kanji. So, for example, in Lesson 16—the first lesson in this book—a total of thirteen characters （手 日 本 一 年 生 四 人 行 口 二 男 女） are used. Learners, however, are not expected to master all thirteen characters at this stage. Instead learners are required to study the characters that appear in the New Kanji list on the first page of every lesson. In Lesson 16, for example, three of the characters used in this lesson （一 四 二） and four other numbers （三 五 六） are introduced as New Kanji.

All New Kanji have been carefully selected according to strict criteria: We have included the basic characters with simple forms or kanji that represent vocabulary that learners already know. Particular care has also been taken in the order in which kanji are introduced in this volume: Where possible we have tried to group together characters of similar meaning thus supporting the sometimes difficult process of kanji acquisition. For example, in Lesson 20, we introduced all seven kanji that are used to write the days of the week in Japanese. Likewise, in Lesson 18, learners will meet three characters （上 下 中） that are used to describe spatial location. Naturally the adoption of this approach means that the number of kanji introduced in each lesson is variable. The maximum number of kanji introduced in any lesson is seven and the minimum is three.

Note that some compounds are partially written with kanji in this book where usually one would expect to see them written with two or three kanji. For example, the compounds 先輩 and 誕生日 are written 先ぱい and たんじょう日, with the kanji not introduced in this volume appearing in hiragana. This reflects our philosophy that at this stage, at least, it is more important to provide the learner with opportunities to recognize any character than it is to adhere to strict rules of Japanese orthography. It also similar to the way kanji is exposed in Japanese elementary-school textbooks, imitating the way in which most native Japanese first learn kanji.

Maximum use has been made of furigana pronunciation guides in this volume to support and develop accurate reading skills: The correct reading in context of each and every character has been printed in kana immediately underneath the character to which it refers. JAPANESE FOR YOUNG PEOPLE II: KANJI WORKBOOK, designed to be used in tandem with this textbook, can be used to study how to read and write all seventy characters introduced in this volume.

Length of Course

As a rule each lesson should take approximately four hours of classroom time to complete. Accordingly this book can form a sixty-hour classroom-based course.

Vocabulary

JAPANESE FOR YOUNG PEOPLE II: STUDENT BOOK introduces a total of approximately four hundred new words including forty-two verbs and thirty-eight adjectives.

Audio Tapes

A set of cassette tapes to accompany this course is available separately and is particularly recommended for review and in learning environments with limited access to natural Japanese as spoken by native speakers. Unlike many cassette tapes, not all the contents of this book has been recorded. As a guide a tape mark indicates all sections recorded on the tapes.

Structure of
JAPANESE FOR YOUNG PEOPLE II: STUDENT BOOK

At the back of the book there is a Grammar Review that summarizes important grammatical information and vocabulary introduced in this volume and a Mini Dictionary that contains two glossaries—Japanese–English and English–Japanese. Both endpapers also provide useful information for all learners. A full and detailed table of the hiragana and katakana scripts has been printed at the front and an annotated map of Japan has been printed at the back.

The Lessons

The table on the next page shows in detail the structure that forms the core of this book.

LESSON	FUNCTION	SITUATION	STRUCTURES, EXPRESSIONS, & VOCABULARY SETS	KANJI
L16 to 18	EXISTENCE & LOCATION Comparison Showing hesitation	*school* *other schools* *railroad station* *in town* *at home*	VERBS 3 (EXISTENCE) 「あります／います」 EXISTENTIAL/LOCATIONAL SENTENCES LOCATION MARKERS （上／下／中／前／後／右／左／隣／近く） COUNTERS（〜階、〜人、〜冊） CONNECTING TWO SENTENCES「……が、……」 「あのう〜」	一 二 三 四 五 六 七 八 九 十 百 千 万 上 下 中 人 子
L19 to 20	STATES Starting a conversation Expressing an opinion	*school* *homestay family* *friend's house* *department store*	ADJECTIVES 2 (MODIFYING PHRASES) ADVERBS OF DEGREE（とても、あまり、全然） 「すみませんが、〜について教えてください」	大 小 犬 田 円 日 月 火 水 木 金 土
L21 to 22	USING THE TELEPHONE GIVING & RECEIVING	*homestay family* *school*	VERBS 4 (GIVING & RECEIVING) (Verbs that take direct/indirect objects)	山 本 男 女 正 先 生 名 前
L23 to 24	POSSESSION OCCURRENCE Asking for information	*homestay family* *school* *after school* *friend's house* *restaurant*	VERBS 5 (POSSESSION & OCCURRENCE) （あります） COUNTERS（〜台） 「〜って何ですか」	雨 何 時 分 半 学 校 休
L25	MAKING INVITATIONS Inviting Accepting/declining invitations	*friend's house* *school* *homestay family*	「〜ませんか」 「(V) 〜ましょうか」 「〜ましょう」	口 目 耳 手 足
L26 to 28	ABILITY/POSSIBILITY/ UNDERSTANDING/ LIKES/PAIN Opening phrases MAKING COMPARISONS	*school* *homestay family* *hospital* *restaurant*	「は」「が」SENTENCES 「〜は〜ができます／わかります／上手です／好きです／痛いです」 「ちょっと いいですか」 どちら 一番	見 読 聞 多 少 好 車 食 飲 早
L29	USING MASS TRANSIT Describing how one gets to a specific destination such as school Talking about periods of time	*school* *railroad station* *post office*	VERBS 6 「〜で〜に乗ります／を降ります」 「〜で〜に着きます／を出ます」 「〜かかります」	行 来 入 出
L30	MAKING A SPEECH Talking about oneself, one's family and one's hometown in a logical structure	*public meeting*	ORDINAL CONNECTIVES 「まず」「次に」「最後に」	年 友 町 村

Grammar Review

Organized into Sentence Patterns, Interrogatives, Adjectives, Verbs, Particles, Adverbs, and Adverbial Phrases, the Grammar Review summarizes the key grammatical structures and vocabulary sets presented in this book.

Mini Dictionary

A full set of glossaries are included in this volume to facilitate self-study and provide all learners with an opportunity to familiarize themselves with using a bilingual dictionary at this preparatory stage. Both a Japanese–English glossary and an English–Japanese glossary are provided so learners can look up English and Japanese words.

Lesson Structure

As the following chart shows, each lesson has been structured to make JAPANESE FOR YOUNG PEOPLE an appropriate course for any classroom situation.

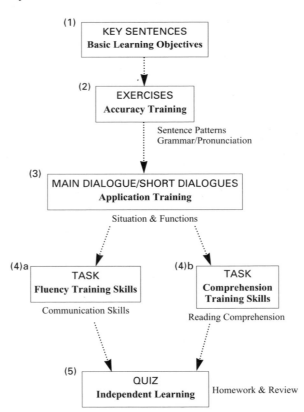

Key Sentences (1)

To indicate the basic learning objectives of each lesson, the principal sentence patterns are presented as example sentences on the first page of that lesson.

New Kanji

A list of all the New Kanji that are introduced in any lesson is printed below the Key Sentences on the first page of that lesson. Learners should refer to JAPANESE FOR YOUNG PEOPLE II: KANJI WORKBOOK for detailed explanations of how to read, use, and write the kanji.

Exercises (2)

All the Exercises in this volume are composed of illustrations and cues or examples in Japanese so that learner progress is not impeded by the mundane task of always having to translate from one language into the other. The first exercises in any lesson introduce key vocabulary necessary to practice the sentence patterns. Thereafter the exercises progress at a realistic pace that facilitates practice in spoken Japanese from simple to more complicated sentences. Each exercise begins with one or more example to give learners a clear idea of what is required from them in that particular exercise. Note that where two examples are provided, the learner has to choose which sample pattern is most appropriate for each question in that exercise.

Main Dialogue/Text (3)

This section aims to provide learners with functional and situational examples of how the sentence patterns introduced in that lesson are actually used in context. Because it is crucial that learners have an immediate grasp of the situation being illustrated, each dialogue or text is introduced with a short sentence in English that effectively describes the circumstances of that dialogue. Dialogues are also illustrated with a comic strip that summarizes the key points of the conversation with an appropriate number of frames. The speech bubbles contain some English words and pictures to help learners guess what is being said and can be put to particularly effective use in role-playing situations that are based around the dialogue. Some dialogues end with a brief summary sentence that is indicated with the ☺ mark. These summaries have been designed not only to help learners describe what is going on in the dialogue but also to explain the conversation objectively as a third party. Learners will find this practice useful in the future when they begin to write in Japanese.

Short Dialogues (3)

Two or three shorter dialogues are included both as applications of usage touched on in the Main Dialogue, or as illustrations of usage not taken up in the Main Dialogue. Note that to familiarize learners with the different levels of speech used in Japanese, dialogues presented in the plain style are also included.

Vocabulary

All new words are presented as they appear after the Key Sentences, Exercises, Main Dialogue/Text, and Short Dialogues sections. Note that the English equivalents provided to enable learners to check meaning and organize vocabulary items are restricted to the meaning and usage of the context in which they appear.

Vocabulary Builder

All the vocabulary presented in JAPANESE FOR YOUNG PEOPLE I: STUDENT BOOK is deemed to be essential vocabulary that should be learned by all students of the Japanese language. At this second stage, however, optional vocabulary grouped together under topics has been included so that learners can select the words that they personally need to know in Japanese. Topics include Animals, Colors, Vegetables, Fruit, Sports, Musical Instruments, Parts of the Body, and Occupations.

Summary Table

Although the lack of any grammatical explanation or linguistic description of sentence patterns is indeed a key feature of this course, we recognize the need for learners to understand the language system as they progress through this book. Accordingly important grammatical areas have been summarized in tabular form at the end of the last lesson in which they are presented. Learners will find Summary Tables for こ－そ－あ－ど, あります／います, Adjectives, and Family expressions.

Japan News

In some lessons learners will find a Japan News article that provides important background information about traditional and contemporary Japanese culture in English, recognizing the emphasis that is often placed on acquiring a deeper understanding of the country whose language is being studied.

Task (4)

With the aim of facilitating more flexible practice of sentence patterns and vocabulary, a Task has been included in some lessons. Some tasks (asking for telephone numbers and addresses, shopping, planning a trip, talking about one's family, hometown or life) provide situational and functional practice and others are included to improve reading comprehension and writing skills.

Quiz (5)

A Quiz is included for each lesson in JAPANESE FOR YOUNG PEOPLE II: KANJI WORKBOOK to enable learners to check progress.

ACKNOWLEDGMENTS

This textbook was written by three AJALT instructors, Sachiko Adachi, Harumi Mizuno, and Mieko Chōsho. They were assisted by Sanae Kimu, Mitsuyoshi Kaji, and Hiroshi Higuchi. Special thanks are due to Hidemi Makino who single-handedly created all the illustrations in this textbook. The authors would also like to thank Paul Hulbert and other editorial staff at Kodansha International for translating and compiling the glossaries, as well as the usual editorial tasks.

Preparation of this textbook was partially assisted with a grant from The Foundation of Language Education.

The photographs reprinted on pages 37 and 43 were taken by Eguchi Juria (girl cleaning blackboard), Hirosaka Toshihiko (on the way home), Kudo Masahiro (baseball), Abe Shinjiro (soccer), Mori Keisuke (sumo wrestling), Nakamoto Itsuko (koto), and Yamazaki Hideyuki (judo). These photographs originally appeared in *The Way We Are: Japanese High School Students' Lives*, a special booklet produced and available from The Japan Forum in Tokyo.

Lesson 16

HERE, THERE, AND OVER THERE

たいいくかんは　どこですか。

KEY SENTENCES

1. ここは　きょうしつです。

2. お手あらいは　そこです。

★ V O C A B U L A R Y ★

ここ	here (See SUMMARY TABLE on p. 8)
（お）手あらい	toilet, lavatory
そこ	there (See SUMMARY TABLE on p. 8)

◆ N E W　K A N J I ◆

一　二　三　四　五　六　七

EXERCISES I

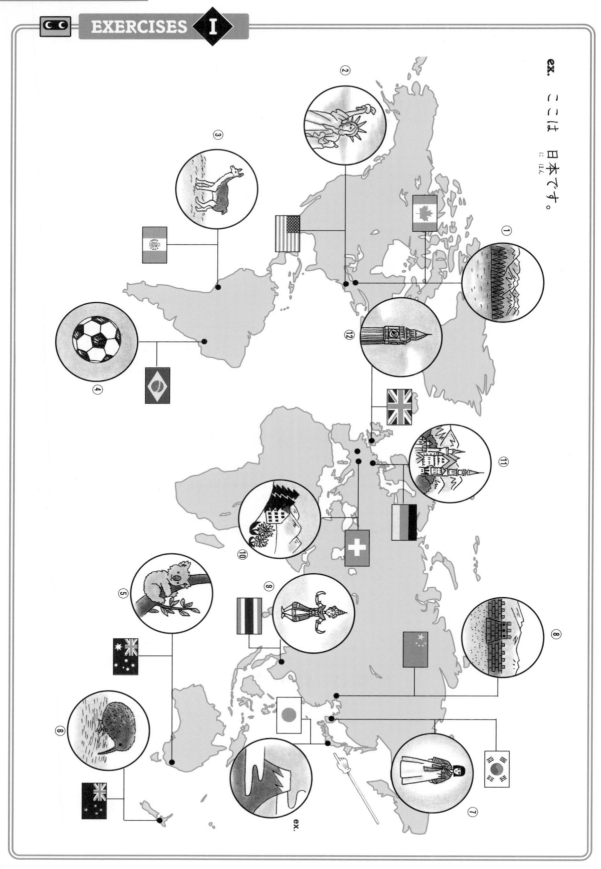

ex. ここは 日本_{にほん}です。

1. ex. 一年生の　きょうしつ
いち ねん せい

ex.

①

②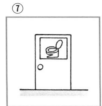

③

④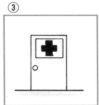

⑤

⑥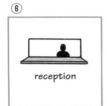

⑦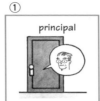

⑧

2. ex. ここは　きょうしつです。

そこは　お手あらいです。
　　　　て

あそこは　プールです。

ex.

①

②

③

EXERCISES Ⅲ

ex. A： お手あらいは　どこですか。

B： ここです。

😊 お手あらいは　ここです。

ex.

①

②

③

一年生 いちねんせい	first-grade school student, first-year pupil
～年生 ねんせい	–grade school student, –year primary pupil
～年 ねん	–grade, –year
こうちょうしつ	principal's office
～しつ	–office, –room
しょくいんしつ	teachers' lounge, staff room
しょくいん	staff
ほけんしつ	medical room, infirmary
としょしつ	library (See NOTE)
コンピュータールーム	computer room
コンピューター	computer
ルーム	room
うけつけ	reception
こうてい	school grounds
あそこ	over there (See SUMMARY TABLE on p. 8)
四かい よん	fourth floor, fourth story
～かい	floor, story (counter)

 You have already learned the word としょかん to mean library in Lesson 11 of JYPI: STUDENT BOOK. This word is used to refer to a building whose sole function is lending books and periodicals. としょしつ, however, is used when one room or one part of a school, college, or company provides library services.

COUNTING: floors

いっかい	一かい	first floor, ground floor*
にかい	二かい	second floor, first floor
さんがい	三がい	third floor, second floor
よにかい	四かい	fourth floor, third floor
ごかい	五かい	fifth floor, fourth floor
ろっかい	六かい	sixth floor, fifth floor
ななかい	七かい	seventh floor, sixth floor
はちかい／はっかい	八かい	eighth floor, seventh floor
きゅうかい	九かい	ninth floor, eighth floor
じゅっかい	十かい	tenth floor, ninth floor
なんがい	何がい	which floor

*Note that the first definition follows US usage and the second definition follows UK usage.

MAIN DIALOGUE

Bādo-kun is visiting another school for a group judo practice. This is the first time that he has been to the school.

バードくん　　　　：　すみません、たいいくかんは　どこですか。

うけつけの　人：　あそこです。まっすぐ　行ってください。
　　　　　　　　　　　　　ひだりです。

バードくん　　　　：　ありがとうございます。

Bādo-kun is standing in front of a door displaying a sign on which something is written in kanji. He thinks it might be the locker rooms, but because he cannot read kanji, he has to ask someone to make sure.

バードくん　　　　：　あのう、ここは　こういしつですか。

男の子　　　　　　：　いいえ、こういしつは　二かいです。

バードくん　　　　：　どうも。

★ VOCABULARY ★

まっすぐ	straight on
行ってください	please go
ひだり	left
あのう	Well …, Excuse me, … (used to express hesitation when about to ask or tell someone something)
こういしつ	locker rooms, changing rooms
どうも	thanks

SHORT DIALOGUES

1

バードくん： すみません。ここは　みなみ口ですか。

男の　人 ： いいえ、きた口ですよ。

バードくん： あ、そうですか。ありがとうございました。

2

バードくん： すみません。しんじゅく行きの　バスていは　どこですか。

女の　人 ： しんじゅく行きですか。あそこですよ。

バードくん： あ、あそこですか。ありがとうございました。

3

バードくん： すみません。しんかんせんの　かいさつ口は　ここですか。

男の　人 ： いいえ、ここは　しんかんせんのではありません。

しんかんせんの　かいさつ口は　ちゅうおう口です。

VOCABULARY

みなみ口	south exit	～行き	bound for–
みなみ	south	バスてい	bus stop
～口	–exit	かいさつ口	ticket gate
きた	north	ちゅうおう口	main entrance and exit
しんじゅく行き	bound for Shinjuku	ちゅうおう	center
しんじゅく	Shinjuku (name of area in Tokyo)		

SUMMARY TABLE

COMPLETE　こ-そ-あ-ど

	こ-words	そ-words	あ-words	ど-words
thing	これ this	それ that	あれ that over there	どれ which
demonstrative	この　本 this book	その　本 that book	あの　本 that book over there	どの　本 which book
place	ここ here	そこ there	あそこ over there	どこ where

DESCRIBING A PHOTOGRAPH

食どうに　おかあさんが　います。
しょく

KEY SENTENCES

1. いまに　テレビが　あります。

2. しょくいんしつに　田中先生が　います。
た　なか せん せい

3. つくえの　上に　はなや　本が　あります。
うえ　　　　　　　ほん

4. こうていに　だれも　いません。

VOCABULARY

に	in (particle)
あります（ある）	is (used for things that cannot move of their own accord, such as books, buildings, plants, vehicles, etc.) (See SUMMARY TABLE on p. 27)
います（いる）	is (used for living things that move, such as people, animals, etc.) (See SUMMARY TABLE on p. 27)
上 うえ	on
だれも　いません	nobody is …

NEW KANJI

八　九　十　百　千　万

⊂⊃ EXERCISES Ⅰ

1. ex. いまに　テーブルが　あります。

2. ex. A：いまに　何_{なに}が　ありますか。

B：テーブルが　あります。

⊂⊃ EXERCISES Ⅱ

1. a. ex. いまに　女の_{おんな}　人_{ひと}が　います。

b. ex. いまに　犬_{いぬ}が　います。

2. a. ex. A：いまに　だれが　いますか。

B：女の_{おんな}　人_{ひと}が　います。

b. ex. A：いまに　何_{なに}が　いますか。

B：犬_{いぬ}が　います。

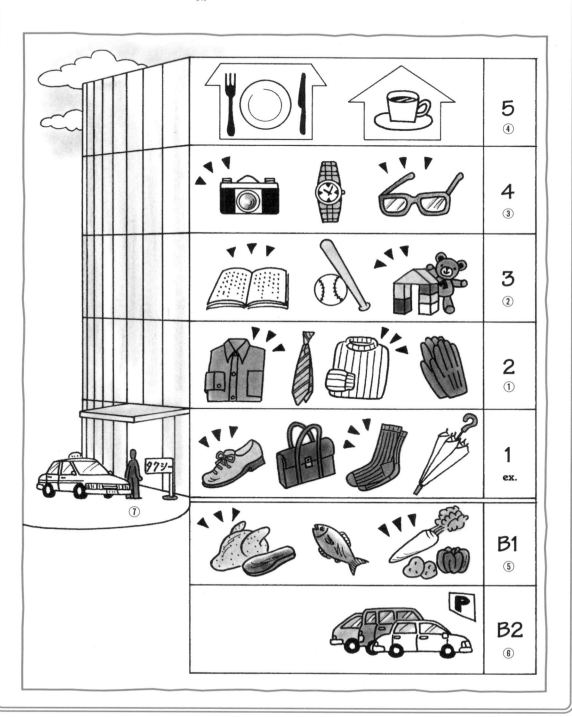

EXERCISES III

1. **ex.** 一かいに くつや くつ下が あります。

2. **ex.** A： 一かいに 何が ありますか。

B： くつや くつ下が あります。

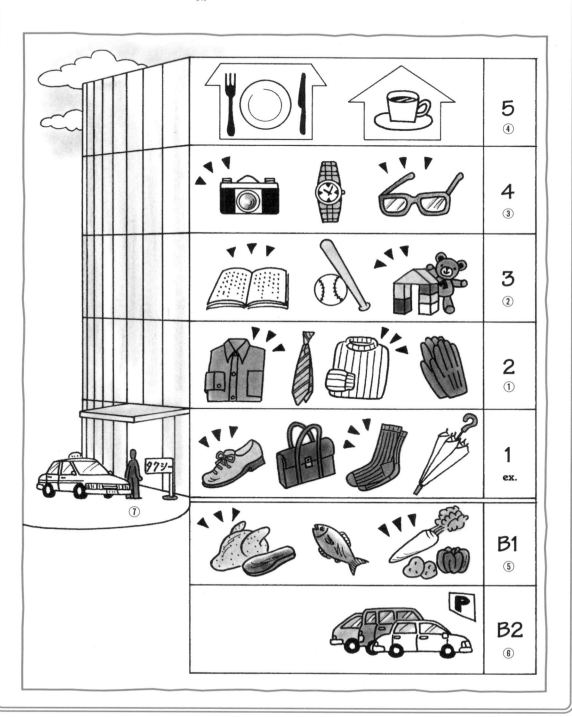

EXERCISES IV

ex. 車の 上に ねこが います。
くるま うえ

EXERCISES V

1. ex. 本だなの 上に えが あります。
ほん　　　うえ

2. ex. A: 本だなの 上に 何が ありますか。
ほん　　　うえ　 なに

B: えが あります。

テーブル	table
ソファー	sofa
犬 いぬ	dog
ねこ	cat
とり	bird
くつ下 した	a sock, (a pair of) socks
おもちゃ	toy
めがね	(eye) glasses, spectacles
ちか	basement
やさい	vegetable
ちゅうしゃじょう	parking lot, car park
げんかん	entrance hall
タクシーのりば	taxi stand, taxi rank
のりば	stand, platform (any place where you board a vehicle)
下 した	under
前 まえ	in front of, before
うしろ	back, behind
中 なか	inside
何も　いません なに	nothing is …
本だな ほん	bookshelf
木 き	tree
何も　ありません なに	nothing is …
ドア	door

CC

VOCABULARY BUILDER 1
Animals

animal	*どうぶつ	lion	ライオン
bird	*とり	monkey	さる
cat	*ねこ	mouse, rat	ねずみ
cow	うし	pig	ぶた
dog	*犬 いぬ	rabbit, hare	うさぎ
elephant	ぞう	sheep	ひつじ
frog	かえる	snake	へび
giraffe	きりん	tiger	とら
horse	うま		

*previously learned vocabulary

Bādo-kun shows Yamamoto-kun a picture of his house in the United States.

これは　バードくんの　うちの　しゃしんです。

食どうに　おかあさんが　います。

いまに　ソファーや　テレビが　あります。

にわに　木や　はなが　あります。にわに　おとうさんと　犬が　います。

だいどころに　だれも　いません。

VOCABULARY

食どう	dining room
にわ	garden
だいどころ	kitchen

SHORT DIALOGUES

1

バードくん ： 山本くんの　うちに　犬が　いる？

山本くん　 ： うん、いるよ。

バードくん ： ねこも　いる？

山本とくん ： ううん、　いない。

2

バードくん ： どこで　コピーを　する。

かとうくん ： コンビニで　する。

バードくん ： こうばんの　となりに　コンビニが　あるよ。

JAPAN NEWS

Japan's reputation as a law-abiding nation is well known the world over. But have you ever thought about why the crime rate is so strikingly low? One answer can be found in Japan's primary mechanism of police deployment: The *koban* or neighborhood sub-station. Use them whenever you think that a police officer might be able to assist you.

Lost in Tokyo? A police officer will be pleased to show you exactly how to reach your destination. Lost and stolen property? Road accidents? The *koban* provides a rapid response to any kind of incident.

The *koban* ensures law and order throughout its jurisdiction. So, if you need assistance, don't hesitate to ask a police officer at your neighborhood *koban*.

VOCABULARY

ううん	no (informal word for いいえ)
いない	is not (informal speech for いません)
コピーを　する	make a copy
コピー	a copy
コンビニ	convenience store
こうばん	police box (See JAPAN NEWS)
となり	next to

でんわは　スーパーの　前
まえ
に　あります。

KEY SENTENCES

1. テーブルの　上
うえ
に　本
ほん
が　たくさん　あります。

2. 本
ほん
やの　前
まえ
に　子
こ
どもが　五人
ごにん
　います。

3. でんわは　スーパーの　前
まえ
に　あります。

4. かとうくんは　おんがくしつに　います。

★ VOCABULARY ★

たくさん	many, a lot of

◆ NEW KANJI ◆

上　下　中　人　子

C C EXERCISES ◆ I

1. ex. りんごが　二つ　あります。
<small>ふた</small>

2. ex. A : りんごが　いくつ　ありますか。

B : 二つ　あります。
<small>ふた</small>

ex.

①

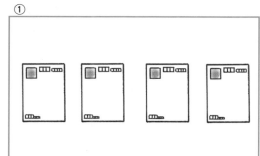

②

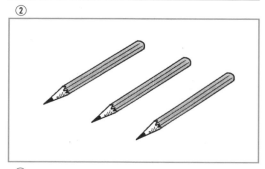

③

④

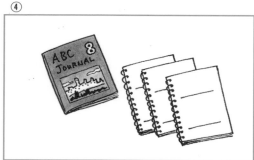

⑤

⑥

⑦

3. ex. テーブルの　上に　りんごが　二つ　あります。
うえ　　　　　　　　　　　ふた

4. ex. A：　どこに　りんごが　ありますか。

B：　テーブルの　上に　あります。
うえ

ex.

①

②

③

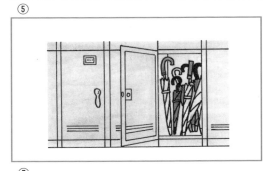

④

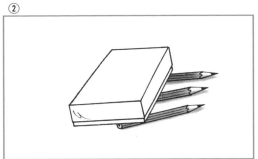

⑤

⑥

⑦

EXERCISES II

1. ex. 男の 子が 一人 います。
<small>おとこ　こ　　ひと り</small>

2. ex. 本やの 前に 男の 子が 一人 います。
<small>ほん　　まえ　おとこ　こ　　ひと り</small>

ex.

①
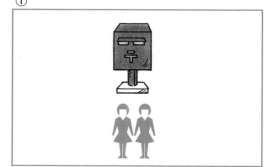

②

③

④
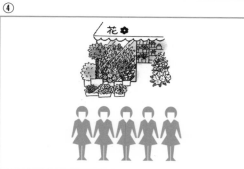

⑤

⑥
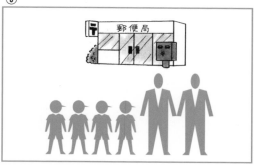

⑦

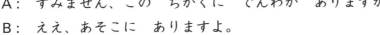

EXERCISES III

ex. A: すみません、この ちかくに でんわが ありますか。

　　B: ええ、あそこに ありますよ。

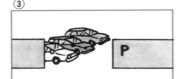

①  ② ③  ④

EXERCISES IV

1. ex. でんわは ぎんこうの 前に あります。

2. ex. A: でんわは どこに ありますか。

　　　　 B: ぎんこうの 前に あります。

3. ex. 本やは ぎんこうの となりに あります。

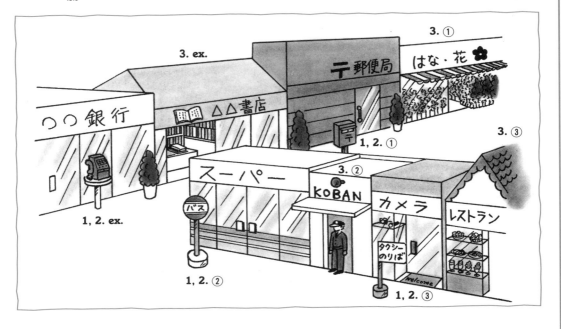

EXERCISES Ⅴ

ex. 先ぱい　　　：　あれっ、かとうくんは？
せん

バードくん：　かとうくんは　しょくいんしつに　います。

ex.

①
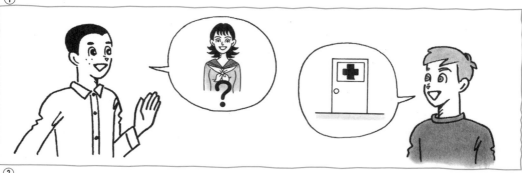

②

③

二さつ _に	two books
〜さつ	(counter for books)
くだもの	fruit
何さつ _{なん}	how many (books)
何人 _{なんにん}	how many (people)
はこ	box
かご	cage, basket
ロッカー	locker
さいふ	wallet, purse
ポスト	mail box, letter box
ちかく	near, close to
あれっ	Oh!, Oh dear! (used as an exclamation of surprise)

COUNTING: people

ひとり	一人	1 person
ふたり	二人	2 people
さんにん	三人	3 people
よにん	四人	4 people
ごにん	五人	5 people
ろくにん	六人	6 people
しちにん	七人	7 people
はちにん	八人	8 people
きゅうにん	九人	9 people
じゅうにん	十人	10 people
なんにん	何人	how many people

MAIN DIALOGUE

Bādo-kun asks a woman where the nearest public telephone can be found.

バードくん：　すみません、この　ちかくに　でんわが　ありますか。

女の　人　：　ええ、ありますよ。

バードくん：　どこですか。

女の　人　：　あそこに　スーパーが　ありますね。
　　　　　　　でんわは　あの　スーパーの　前です。

バードくん：　どうも　ありがとうございました。

😊　でんわは　スーパーの　前に　あります。

SHORT DIALOGUES

1

田中先生 ： そうじの　じかんです。みんな　いますか。
（たなかせんせい）

バードくん： かとうくんが　いません。

田中先生 ： かとうくんは　どこですか。
（たなかせんせい）

山本くん ： お手あらいです。
（やまもと）　　　（て）

2

木村さん ： バードくんの　おとうさんは　日本に　いる？
（きむら）　　　　　　　　　　　　　　　　（にほん）

バードくん： ううん、いないよ。

木村さん ： どこに　いる。
（きむら）

バードくん： アメリカに　いる。

3

みどりちゃん： ただいま。

バードくん ： おかえりなさい。

みどりちゃん： あれっ、おかあさんが　いない。おやつは？

バードくん ： れいぞうこに　あるよ。ほら。

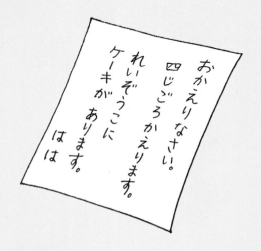

おかえりなさい。
四じごろかえります。
れいぞうこに
ケーキが　あります。
はは

✪ V O C A B U L A R Y ✪

じかん	time
みんな	everybody
おやつ	afternoon snack
れいぞうこ	refrigerator, fridge
ほら	Look! (used to get someone's attention)

SUMMARY TABLE •

あります／います

Present Form		Past Form	
aff.	*neg.*	*aff.*	*neg.*
あります	ありません	ありました	ありませんでした
います	いません	いました	いませんでした

JAPAN NEWS

In Japan the Chinese zodiac of twelve animals is sometimes used to express the year. The Chinese zodiac was first adopted for use in Japan in the sixth century and until the Meiji Restoration (1868) it was also used to tell the time and map out direction like the points of the compass. Some people believe that your personality can be influenced by the character of the animal that is used to represent the year of your birth. For example, 1999 was the year of the rabbit or hare. A person born in this year is supposed to be fickle. Do you know which animal is used to represent the year of your birth? Use the chart on the right to find out your Chinese zodiac sign.

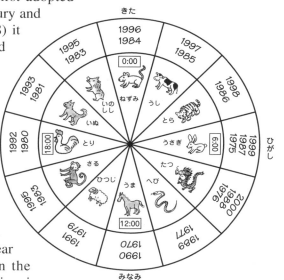

T A S K ⑪

へびは どこに いますか。

Spot the difference! Study the two pictures below and see if you can find five differences. First write them down in the spaces provided using the verb います and then describe the differences to a friend or partner. The Vocabulary Builder on page 13 will help you find the Japanese names for the animals that you have not yet learned.

ex.

ひだりの えでは <u>へびは 車の 上に</u> いますが、

みぎ*¹の えでは <u>車の 下に</u> います。

*¹みぎ right

LET'S TRY!

1. ひだりの えでは _____

みぎの えでは _____

2. ひだりの えでは _____

みぎの えでは _____

3. ひだりの えでは _____

みぎの えでは _____

4. ひだりの えでは _____

みぎの えでは _____

5. ひだりの えでは _____

みぎの えでは _____

学校は　たのしいです。
がっ　こう

but interesting

KEY SENTENCES

1. 学校は　たのしいです。
がっ　こう

2. 友だちは　とても　しんせつです。
とも

3. 日本ごは　むずかしくないです。
に　ほん

4. ここは　しずかではありません。

5. かんじは　少し　むずかしいですが、おもしろいです。
すこ

☆ V O C A B U L A R Y ☆

たのしい	enjoyable (－い adj.)
むずかしくないです	… is not difficult
むずかしい	difficult (－い adj.)
しずかではありません	… is not quiet

◆ N E W　K A N J I ◆

大　　小　　犬　　田　　円

C C EXERCISES Ⅰ

ex. バードくんの　本
ほん

①
2,000yen

②

③

④
new

⑤
interesting

⑥
famous

⑦
beautiful

C C EXERCISES Ⅱ

1. a. ex.　クラブ

ex.

①

②

③

b. ex.　食べもの
た

ex.

①

②

③

2. a. ex. ながい　えんぴつ　　みじかい　えんぴつ

ex.
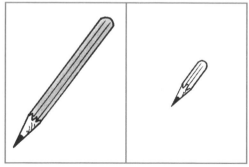

①

②

③

④

⑤

⑥

⑦

⑧

enjoyable

b. ex.　きれいな　はな

ex.

pretty

①

famous

②

quiet

③

kind

④

convenient

EXERCISES III

1. ex.　この　えんぴつは　ながいです。
　　　　この　えんぴつは　みじかいです。

ex.

①
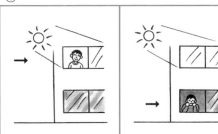

②

③

④
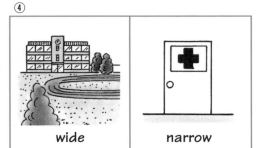
wide　　　narrow

⑤

⑥

enjoyable

2. ex. さくらは　きれいです。

ex.

pretty

①

famous

②

quiet

③

convenient

④

kind

EXERCISES IV

1. ex. バイクは　はやいです。

じてん車は　はやくないです。

ex.

◯　　fast　　✕

①
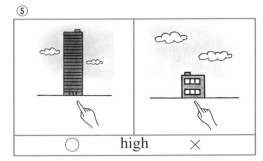
◯　　wide　　✕

②
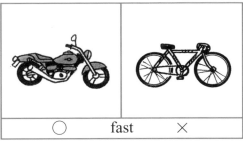
◯　　long　　✕

③
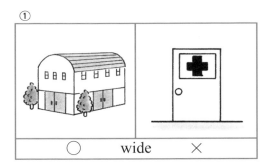
◯　　difficult　　✕

④

◯　　good　　✕

⑤
◯　　high　　✕

2. ex. ほけんしつは　しずかです。

　　　　 たいいくかんは　しずかではありません。

ex.

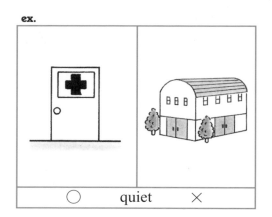

⃝　quiet　✕

①

⃝　kind　✕

②

⃝　famous　✕

③

⃝　tidy　✕

④

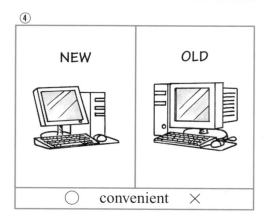

⃝　convenient　✕

1. ex. 田中先生 　：　サッカーは　おもしろいですか。
た　なかせんせい

バードくん：　はい、おもしろいです。

ex.

①

②

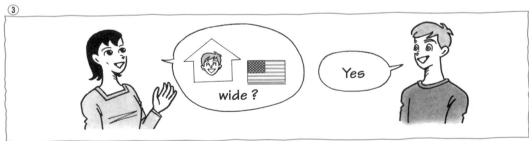

③

④

2. ex.　バードくん：　テストは　むずかしいですか。

　　　　　田中先生　　：　いいえ、むずかしくないです。
　　　　　た　なか せん せい

ex.

ex. かんじは　おもしろいですが、むずかしいです。

ex.

interesting

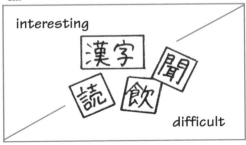

difficult

① fast

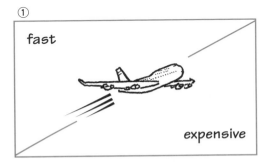

expensive

② quiet

not clean

③ cheap

not delicious

④ narrow

bright

JAPAN NEWS

Most Japanese schoolchildren at junior high have to wear a uniform to school every day. In most public schools, the uniform for girls is loosely based on a traditional sailor's kit and is generally known as *sērā-fuku* or "sailor's clothes." For boys, too, the all-black suit with high Prussian collar has military overtones, perhaps something like that worn by European soldiers in the late nineteenth century.

At private or independent schools, you will see a greater variety of uniforms. Boys often wear suits or blazers and flannels with a school tie. Girls may have a choice of pleated plaid or tartan skirts. One thing, however, is sure: School uniforms are fashionable in Japan. Girls, in particular, have been known to select their junior high based on its uniform.

EXERCISES VII

ex. 山本くんの　おかあさん：学校は　どうですか。
　　　　　　バードくん　　　　　：たのしいです。

ex.

①

②

③

④

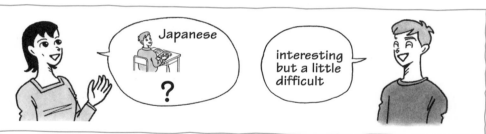

クラブ	school club, extracurricular activity
せいふく	school uniform
食べもの	food, things to eat
飲みもの	drinks, things to drink
のりもの	transport
たてもの	building
ながい	long (− い adj.)
みじかい	short (− い adj.)
ひろい	wide (− い adj.)
せまい	narrow (− い adj.)
ふるい	old (− い adj.)
あかるい	bright (− い adj.)
くらい	dark (− い adj.)
きれい （な）	tidy (− な adj.)
やさしい	easy (− い adj.)
おそい	slow (− い adj.)
はやい	fast (− い adj.)
たかい	high (− い adj.)
ひくい	low (− い adj.)
べんり （な）	convenient (− な adj.)
なつ休み	summer vacation
〜休み	vacation, holiday
ふゆ	winter

JAPAN NEWS

The Japanese study a variety of subjects during their three years of compulsory education at junior high or middle school. As well as mathematics, science, Japanese language and some of the other subjects that were studied at elementary school, schoolchildren begin learning English as a foreign language for the first time.

The school year in Japan starts in April and not September or January like many other countries. The first semester runs, therefore, from April through mid-July, the second semester from September through late December, and the third semester from early January through mid-March. At present, many schools are also open on two or three Saturdays every month, but from the year 2000 most public schools, at least, will reduce teaching time to five days per week.

If you go to a Japanese school, you may be surprised by the amount of homework that is given every day. Even first-grade elementary pupils have a good hour's worth of homework every night. Worst of all is the vast amount of homework set for the long summer vacation.

MAIN DIALOGUE

Yamamoto-kun's mother is asking Bādo-kun about his school life.

山本くんの　おかあさん：　バードくん、学校は　たのしいですか。
やまもと　　　　　　　　　　　　　　　　がっこう

バードくん　　　　　　　　：　はい、たのしいです。
　　　　　　　　　　　　　　　みんな　とても　しんせつです。

山本くんの　おかあさん：　べんきょうは　どうですか。
やまもと

バードくん　　　　　　　　：　すうがくや　おんがくは　おもしろいで
　　　　　　　　　　　　　　　すが、かんじは　少し　むずかしいです。
　　　　　　　　　　　　　　　　　　　　すこ

VOCABULARY

どうですか	How is it?
どう	how

SHORT DIALOGUES

1

バードくん： 先生の うちは 学校から とおいですか。
せんせい　　　　　　　　がっこう

田中先生 ： いいえ、とおくないです。 バスで 二十分ぐらいです。
た なか せん せい　　　　　　　　　　　　　　　　　　　　　に じゅっぷん

バードくん： そうですか。 ちかいですね。

2

山本くん ： バードくんの 犬は 大きい？
やま もと　　　　　　　　　　いぬ　　おお

バードくん： ううん、小さいよ。 とっても かわいいよ。
ちい

⭐ VOCABULARY ⭐

とおい	far (－い adj.)
ちかい	near (－い adj.)
二十分ぐらい にじゅっぷん	about 20 minutes
～ぐらい	about
そうですか	I see. (See NOTE)
とっても	very (more informal than とても)
かわいい	cute (－い adj.)

NOTE When そうですか means "I see," as here, it is said with falling intonation. It can also mean "Oh, really?" or "Is that so?" and be a question expecting an answer. In that case, it is said with rising intonation.

JAPAN NEWS

Extracurricular activities play an important part in school life in Japan. Many children join a club or circle at their school that coincides with an interest or hobby that they may have. Some clubs are for sports, such as baseball or soccer, volleyball or basketball. Others are set up to practice some of Japan's traditional martial arts—judo, karate, or kendo. Then there are art clubs, calligraphy societies, groups for trainspotters, and even science clubs at school. Most schools even have a club devoted to English conversation practice, called "English Speaking Society" or ESS for short. Mike Bird is in the school judo club. If you went to a Japanese junior high, what club do you think that you would join?

T A S K ⑫

学校は　どうですか。
がっこう

Use the adjectives listed below to ask your friend or partner questions about their school life. Put a ○ in the parentheses provided for a "yes" answer and a × for a "no" answer. The following example dialogue shows you how to conduct your interview in Japanese.

ex. バードくん：　すみません、学校に　ついて*¹　おしえてください*²。
がっこう

たいいくかんは　大きいですか。
おお

スミスさん：　はい、大きいです。
おお

バードくん：　あたらしいですか。

スミスさん：　いいえ、あたらしくないです。

バードくん：　そうですか。ありがとうございました。

*¹ 〜に　ついて　　　about …
*² おしえてください　Please tell me ….

LET'S INTERVIEW!

ex. たいいくかん　　（ ○ ）big　　　　（ X ）new

1. きょうしつ　　　（　）wide　　　　（　）clean

2. べんきょう　　　（　）interesting　（　）difficult

3. 友だち　　　　　（　）kind
とも

4. クラブ　　　　　（　）enjoyable

5. ひる休み　　　　（　）long
やす

6. としょしつ　　　（　）quiet　　　　（　）convenient

7. 先生　　　　　　（　）friendly
せんせい

8. しゅくだい　　　（　）easy

おまつりは　たのしかったです。

KEY SENTENCES

1. パーティーは　たのしかったです。

2. はな火は　とても　きれいでした。

3. えいがは　ぜんぜん　おもしろくなかったです。

4. かとうくんは　きのう　げんきではありませんでした。

VOCABULARY

たのしかったです	was enjoyable （See SUMMARY TABLE on p. 52）
はな火	fireworks
きれいでした	was beautiful
おもしろくなかったです	was not interesting
げんきではありませんでした	was not well
ぜんぜん…くなかったです	… (not) at all

NEW KANJI

日　月　火　水　木　金　土

EXERCISES I

ex. あつい 日 さむい 日
ひ　　　　　ひ

ex.

①

②

EXERCISES II

1. ex. おまつり

2. ex. パーティーは　たのしかったです。

3. ex. はな火は　きれいでした。
ひ

1. ex. 　① 　② 　③

2. ex. 　① おきなわ 　② ほっかいどう 　③

enjoyable　　hot　　cold　　good

3. ex. 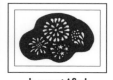　① 　② 　③

beautiful　　lively　　kind　　quiet

1. ex. しあいは　おもしろかったですが、
れんしゅうは　おもしろくなかったです。

ex.

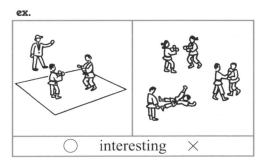

○　interesting　×

①

○　cold　×

②

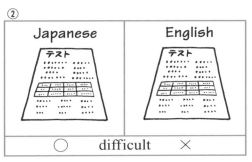

○　difficult　×

③

○　good　×

2. ex. バードくんは　げんきでしたが、
かとうくんは　げんきではありませんでした。

ex.

○　well　×

①

○　lively　×

②

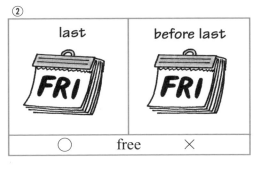

○　free　×

③

○　tidy　×

EXERCISES Ⅳ

1. ex. 田中先生　：パーティーは　たのしかったですか。
たなかせんせい

バードくん：はい、たのしかったです。

ex.

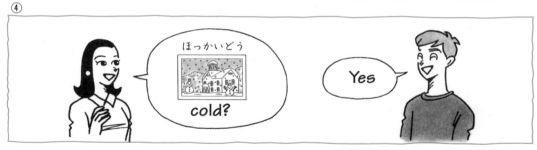

2. ex. 田中先生 ： テストは　むずかしかったですか。
たなかせんせい

　　　　バードくん： いいえ、むずかしくなかったです。

ex.

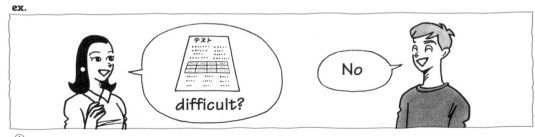

①

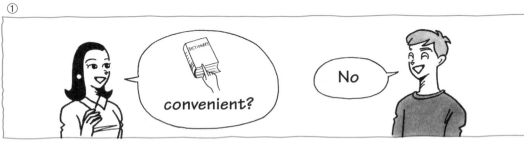

②

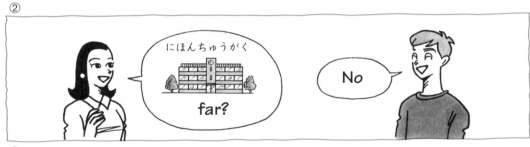

③

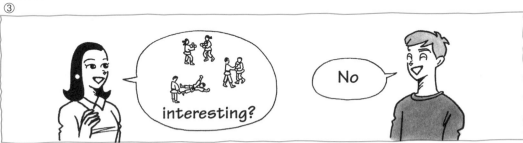

④

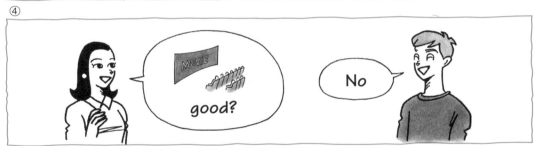

EXERCISES V

ex. すうがくは　とても　むずかしいです。

りかは　あまり　むずかしくないです。

えいごは　ぜんぜん　むずかしくないです。

		very	not very	not at all
ex.	difficult	2πr²		English
①	beautiful			
②	cold	yesterday	the day before yesterday	last week

EXERCISES VI

ex. 1　バードくん：きのう　はな火を　みました。

田中先生　：はな火は　どうでしたか。

バードくん：とても　きれいでした。

田中先生　：それは　よかったですね。

ex. 2　木村さん：しゅうまつに　うみへ　行きました。

田中先生：うみは　どうでしたか。

木村さん：あまり　きれいではありませんでした。

田中先生：それは　ざんねんでしたね。

ex.1

ex.2

★ V O C A B U L A R Y ★

あつい	hot (ー い adj.)
日 _ひ	day
さむい	cold (ー い adj.)
いそがしい	busy (ー い adj.)
ひま（な）	free, not busy (ー な adj.)
にぎやか（な）	lively (ー な adj.)
（お）まつり	festival
しあい	competition
おきなわ	Okinawa (name of island group south of Kyushu)
せんせんしゅう	the week before last
しゅうまつ	weekend
それは　よかったですね。	That's nice.
それは　ざんねんでしたね。	That's a pity.
ざんねん（な）	regrettable (ー な adj.)

SUMMARY TABLE ●

ADJECTIVES

ー い adj.	小さい　じしょ _{ちい}	small dictionary
ー な adj.	べんりな　じしょ	handy dictionary

	Present Form		Past Form	
	aff.	*neg.*	*aff.*	*neg.*
ー い adj.	小さいです _{ちい}	小さくないです _{ちい}	小さかったです _{ちい}	小さくなかったです _{ちい}
ー な adj.	べんりです	べんりではありません	べんりでした	べんりではありませんでした

JAPAN NEWS

Matsuri are essentially native Japanese festivals of Shinto origin held annually on established dates. There are solemn *matsuri* and boisterous occasions featuring games and entertainment. Elaborate festivals flourish in the big cities and small-scale ones in more personal settings or in small communities. Some *matsuri* are performed in a very traditional way, and some have been adapted to modern times.

Many Japanese festivals feature a parade of *mikoshi* (portable shrines) and contests or games that provide opportunities for community members to play together and match skills. Most *matsuri* also include a kind of market or bazaar with colorful stalls that sell tasty snacks, Japanese-style candy, traditional toys, and other goods that can only be bought at a *matsuri*.

Famous festivals include the Sapporo Snow Festival in early February, Hakata Dontaku, held on May 4–5 in Kyushu, the Gion Festival, held in Kyoto on July 17, and the Nebuta Festival, held in Aomori prefecture on August 1–7.

Tanaka-sensē is asking Bādo-kun about the matsuri.

田中先生 ： おまつりは どうでしたか。
た なか せん せい

バードくん： たのしかったです。 小さい みせが たくさん
ありました。木の おもちゃを かいました。
き

田中先生 ： はな火を 見ましたか。
た なか せん せい び み

バードくん： はい、見ました。 とても きれいでした。
み

😊 バードくんは おまつりを 見ました。
み

おまつりは たのしかったです。

小さい みせで 木の おもちゃを かいました。
ちい き

はな火は とても きれいでした。
び

木き	wood

SHORT DIALOGUES

1

バードくん ： きのうの　えいがは　おもしろかった？

山本くん　 ： ううん、ぜんぜん　おもしろくなかった。
やまもと

2

田中先生　 ： しゅうまつの　しあいは　どうでしたか。
たなかせんせい

バードくん ： だめでした。

田中先生　 ： それは　ざんねんでしたね。
たなかせんせい

VOCABULARY

| だめ（な） | no good（－な adj.） |

友だちに でんわを します。
とも

KEY SENTENCES

1. バードくんは おとうさんに 手がみを かきました。
て

2. バードくんは 山本くんの うちに でんわを しました。
やま もと

3. わたしは えきで 友だちに あいます。
とも

VOCABULARY

に	to (indirect object marker, particle)
でんわを します	make a phone call
（でんわを する）	
あいます（あう）	meet

NEW KANJI

山　本　男　女

EXERCISES I

1. ex. カード

ex.

①

②

③

④

2. ex. あいます

ex.

①

② ……？   …… 。

ex. バードくん ： りょうしんです。

田中先生 ： ごりょうしんは　おげんきですか。
<small>た　なか せん せい</small>

バードくん： はい、ありがとうございます。とても　げんきです。

ex. バードくんは　みどりちゃんに　カードを　かきます。

Yamamoto-kun's parents

1. ex. バードくん： わたしは　きのう　ちちに　手がみを　かきました。

ex.	yesterday	
①	everynight 8:00	friend
②	yesterday	
③	last week	
④	the day before yesterday	
⑤	always	聞 飲 ?
⑥	yesterday	address friend

2. ex. A： 田中先生は　だれに　手がみを　かきましたか。

B： かとうくんの　ごりょうしんに　かきました。

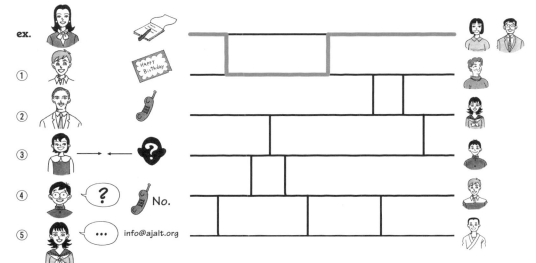

④ No.

⑤ info@ajalt.org

EXERCISES V

ex. 1. A： かとうくんは　よく　友だちに　でんわを　しますか。
　　　　　B： はい、よく　します。

ex. 2. A： みどりちゃんは　よく　友だちに　でんわを　しますか。
　　　　　B： いいえ、あまり　しません。

☆ V O C A B U L A R Y ☆

カード	card
年がじょう	New Year's card
ファックスばんごう	fax number
ファックス	fax
じゅうしょ	address
E（イー）メール　アドレス	e-mail address （Note that for e-mail addresses, the Japanese じゅうしょ is never used.）
E（イー）メール	e-mail
聞きます（聞く）	ask
おしえます（おしえる）	tell
りょうしん	my parents (See SUMMARY TABLE below)
ごりょうしん	(someone else's) parents
きょうだい	brothers and sisters
ごきょうだい	(someone else's) brothers and sisters
そふ	my grandfather
おじいさん	(someone else's) grandfather
そぼ	my grandmother
おばあさん	(someone else's) grandmother
ファックスを　します（ファックスを　する）	send a fax

SUMMARY TABLE •

FAMILY

	OWN	SOMEONE ELSE'S
family	かぞく	ごかぞく
parents	りょうしん	ごりょうしん
father	ちち	おとうさん
mother	はは	おかあさん
grandfather	そふ	おじいさん
grandmother	そぼ	おばあさん
brothers and sisters	きょうだい	ごきょうだい
older brother	あに	おにいさん
older sister	あね	おねえさん
younger brother	おとうと	おとうとさん
younger sister	いもうと	いもうとさん

MAIN DIALOGUE

Bādo-kun calls Yamamoto-kun.

バードくん　　　　　　　：　もしもし、山本さんの　おたくですか。

山本くんの　おかあさん：　はい、そうです。

バードくん　　　　　　　：　バードですが、あきらくんは　いますか。

山本くんの　おかあさん：　いいえ、いま　じゅくです。
　　　　　　　　　　　　　　　　　七時ごろ　かえりますよ。

バードくん　　　　　　　：　そうですか。
　　　　　　　　　　　　　　　　　では　また　よる　でんわを　します。

山本くんの　おかあさん：　はい、おねがいします。

バードくん　　　　　　　：　しつれいします。

山本くんの　おかあさん：　さようなら。

☺　バードくんは　山本くんの　うちに　でんわを　しましたが、
　　山本くんは　いませんでした。　バードくんは　また　よる
　　でんわを　します。

VOCABULARY

もしもし	hello (chiefly used on the telephone)
おたく	(someone else's) home
が	(particle) (See NOTE 1)
あきら	Akira (given name) (See NOTE 2)
じゅく	cram school
また	again
よる	night
おねがいします	Please (do).
しつれいします	Goodbye. (lit. I'm going to be rude [and ring off].)

① Hello. The Yamamoto home?

② Yes it is.

③ This is Mike Bird. ?

④ Now About 7:00.

⑤ I see. Then I'll call again this evening.

⑥ Yes, please do.

⑦ Goodbye.

⑧ Goodbye.

 You learned in Lesson 19 that the particle が means "but" when connecting two sentences. Here, although it is indeed a connecting word, が does not contain any special meaning. It is used simply to create a short pause between the two phrases.

 You learned in the first book that it is usual to call Japanese people by their surnames with a suffix, such as 〜さん or 〜くん. Here, however, Mike refers to his friend by his given name, Akira, because everyone who lives at the Yamamoto household is supposedly called "Yamamoto-san." This is one example of how the names that we call people change according to the circumstances, a common feature of Japanese.

SHORT DIALOGUES

1

バードくん　：　もしもし、山本さんの　おたくですか。

男の　人　：　いいえ、ちがいます。

バードくん　：　あっ、しつれいしました。

男の　人　：　いいえ、どういたしまして。

2

女の　人　：　とうきょう中学校でございます。

バードくん　：　せいとの　バードですが、田中先生を　おねがいします。

女の　人　：　しょうしょう　おまちください。

3

かとうくん　：　きのう　こうちょう先生に　あいました。

先ぱい　：　どこで。

かとうくん　：　ゲームセンターの　前で。　びっくりしました。

VOCABULARY

ちがいます（ちがう）	That's wrong.
あっ	ah
しつれいしました	I'm sorry. (See NOTE on p. 68)
とうきょう中学校でございます	This is Tokyo Junior High School.
とうきょう中学校	Tokyo Junior High School
でございます	is (very polite word for です)
田中先生を　おねがいします	May I speak to Ms. Tanaka?
～を　おねがいします	please …
ゲームセンター	game arcade
びっくりします（びっくりする）	be surprised

T A S K ⑬

ゆき子さんの　じゅうしょを　聞きました。

Study the pictures below and make sentences in Japanese that describe what is happening in the pictures in the right order.

Mike Bird got a letter from his grandmother in the U.S. This made him so happy that he called her soon after getting it.

ex. ① おばあさんは　バードくんに　手がみを　かきました。

② バードくんは　おばあさんの　手がみを　読みました。

③ そして　バードくんは　おばあさんに　でんわを　しました。

Mike Bird has a crush on Yukiko and wants to know her address and telephone number. What do you think he did? Study the pictures below and on the next page and then make sentences in Japanese that describe what happens in the order that it happens.

1. ① _____

② _____

③ そして _____

六十七　67

2. ① _____

② ゆき子^{*1}さんは　バードくんの　手がみが　よく　分かりませんでした。

③ _____

④　とうとう^{*2} _____

^{*1}ゆき子　　Yukiko (given name)
^{*2}とうとう　finally, at last

 In the Main Dialogue on p. 64, しつれいします was used to mean "goodbye." Basically the word しつれい means something akin to "impoliteness" or "bad manners." You can use it with the literal meaning of "I'm going to do something that isn't polite," in situations such as crossing in front of someone, entering the teacher's lounge, and generally getting in someone's way. In the above dialogue, because Mike is apologizing for phoning the wrong number—something that he has already done—he uses the past form しつれいしました。

友だちに　ぼうしを　もらいました。
<small>とも</small>

KEY SENTENCES

1. 木村さんは　バードくんに　ノートを　あげました。
   <small>き　むら</small>

2. バードくんは　木村さんに　ノートを　もらいました。
   <small>き　むら</small>

★ VOCABULARY ★

に	from (indirect object marker, particle) (See NOTE)
あげます（あげる）	give
もらいます（もらう）	receive

◆ NEW KANJI ◆

先　生　正　名　前

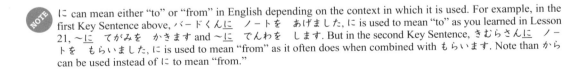

NOTE　に can mean either "to" or "from" in English depending on the context in which it is used. For example, in the first Key Sentence above, バードくん<u>に</u>　ノートを　あげました, に is used to mean "to" as you learned in Lesson 21, ～<u>に</u>　てがみを　かきます and ～<u>に</u>　でんわを　します. But in the second Key Sentence, きむらさん<u>に</u>　ノートを　もらいました, に is used to mean "from" as it often does when combined with もらいます. Note than から can be used instead of に to mean "from."

EXERCISES I

1. ex. プレゼント

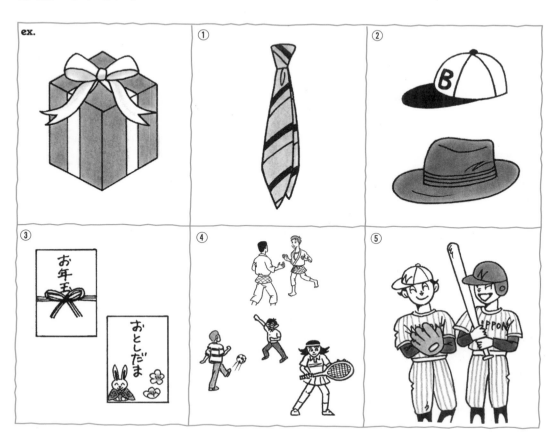

2. ex. あげます

1. ex. バードくんは　はなを　あげます。

木村さんは　はなを　もらいます。

ex.

①

②

③

2. ex. バードくんは　木村さんに　きれいな　はなを　あげます。

木村さんは　バードくんに　きれいな　はなを　もらいます。

ex.

①

②

③

1. **ex. 1** おとうさんは　みどりちゃんに　木の　おもちゃを　あげました。

   ex. 2 バードくんは　おばあさんに　ながい　手がみを　もらいました。

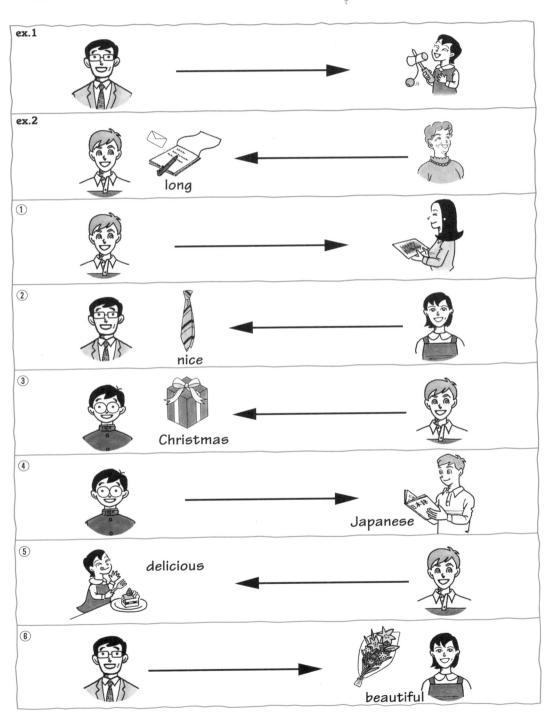

ex.1

ex.2　long

①

② nice

③ Christmas

④ Japanese

⑤ delicious

⑥ beautiful

2. ex. 1　おとうさんは　だれに　木の　おもちゃを　あげましたか。

ex. 2　だれが　おばあさんに　ながい　手がみを　もらいましたか。

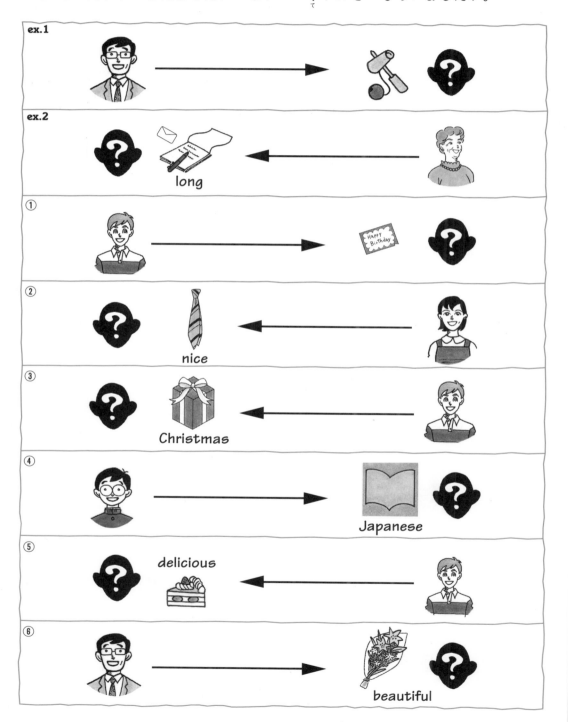

ex.1

ex.2　long

①

② nice

③ Christmas

④ Japanese

⑤ delicious

⑥ beautiful

☆V☆O☆C☆A☆B☆U☆L☆A☆R☆Y☆

プレゼント	present, gift
ネクタイ	tie
ぼうし	cap, hat
お年だま	a New Year's gift
スポーツ	sport
やきゅう	baseball
すてき（な）	nice, fine, wonderful（ー な adj.）
クリスマス	Christmas

JAPAN NEWS

People send New Year's cards to their friends, relatives, and colleagues to express their New Year's resolutions as well as to give updates on their lives. Many take a particular pride in designing and printing their own unique cards, often incorporating a family photograph of a wedding, new baby, or summer holiday or perhaps a colorful illustration of the New Year's animal from the Chinese Zodiac.

It is generally thought best for *nengajō* to arrive on January 1st, and this means that there is usually a mad end-of-year rush to get your cards out on time. A few thoughts for Japan's postal workers who even have to work New Year's Day while the rest of the nation rests and celebrates.

MAIN DIALOGUE

Tanaka-sensē comments about Bādo-kun's baseball cap.

田中先生　　：　すてきな　ぼうしですね。
たなかせんせい

バードくん：　たんじょう日に　かとうくんたちに　もらいました。
　　　　　　　　　び

田中先生　　：　やきゅうの　ぼうしですか。
たなかせんせい

バードくん：　はい、わたしの　好きな　チームの　ぼうしです。
　　　　　　　　　　　　　す

田中先生　　：　いいですね。
たなかせんせい

☺　バードくんは　たんじょう日に　かとうくんたちに　ぼうしを
　　　　　　　　　　　　　　び

　　もらいました。　かとうくんたちは　たんじょう日に　バード
　　　　　　　　　　　　　　　　　　　　　　　　　　び

　　くんに　ぼうしを　あげました。

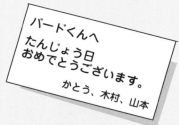

バードくんへ
たんじょう日
おめでとうございます。
　　かとう、木村、山本

☆ VOCABULARY ☆

かとうくんたち	Kato and the others
～たち	(plural suffix used for people)
好き（な） す	likable, favorite (－な adj.)
チーム	team

SHORT DIALOGUES

1

バードくん　　：いつ　お年だまを　もらう。

みどりちゃん：お正月。

バードくん　　：おとうさんも　もらう？

みどりちゃん：ううん、子どもだけ。　おとうさんから　もらうの。

2

バードくん：かわいい　ねこだね。

木村さん　　：ええ、となりの　おばさんに　もらったの。

バードくん：名前は？

木村さん　　：たま。

JAPAN NEWS

All good Japanese children look forward to receiving *otoshidama* on New Year's Day. The *otoshidama* comes in a smart paper envelope like the one illustrated on this page. Inside the lucky child will find a gift of cash. In Japan it is bad manners not to wrap a gift of money and there are many kinds of envelopes specially made for this purpose.

　　How much money do Japanese kids get on New Year's Day? Well that all depends on their age and surroundings. At the time this book went into press, junior high school kids receive an average of 10,000 yen from their parents, relatives, and other family friends.

VOCABULARY

もらう	receive (informal for もらいます)
（お）正月	New Year's Day
だけ	only
から	from (particle) (See NOTE on p. 69)
の	I tell you. (particle in female speech)
となりの　おばさん	the woman next door
もらった	received (informal for もらいました)
たま	Tama (common name for a cat)

T A S K ⑭

クリスマスに　何を　あげますか。
<small>なに</small>

Christmas is coming. The space under the Christmas tree is already packed with yuletide gifts. Jeff has yet to decide what he's going to get the other people in his family this year and so he's keen to know what they have got for one another. He takes a look at the presents and thinks about making a list of what there is. But what if someone was to see the list? No problem. Jeff studies Japanese at school and nobody at home would be able to read anything that he had written in kana and kanji.

Imagine that you are Jeff: Study the picture and take notes in Japanese. The first one has been done for you.

ex. 1 ちちは　ははに　ネックレス^{*1}を　あげます。

2 ははは　ちちに　ネックレスを　もらいます。

① 1 ＿＿＿＿＿＿＿＿＿＿＿＿＿＿＿＿＿＿＿＿＿＿＿＿＿＿＿

2 ＿＿＿＿＿＿＿＿＿＿＿＿＿＿＿＿＿＿＿＿＿＿＿＿＿＿＿

② 1 ＿＿＿＿＿＿＿＿＿＿＿＿＿＿＿＿＿＿＿＿＿＿＿＿＿＿＿

2 ＿＿＿＿＿＿＿＿＿＿＿＿＿＿＿＿＿＿＿＿＿＿＿＿＿＿＿

③ 1 ＿＿＿＿＿＿＿＿＿＿＿＿＿＿＿＿＿＿＿＿＿＿＿＿＿＿＿

2 ＿＿＿＿＿＿＿＿＿＿＿＿＿＿＿＿＿＿＿＿＿＿＿＿＿＿＿

④ 1 ＿＿＿＿＿＿＿＿＿＿＿＿＿＿＿＿＿＿＿＿＿＿＿＿＿＿＿

2 ＿＿＿＿＿＿＿＿＿＿＿＿＿＿＿＿＿＿＿＿＿＿＿＿＿＿＿

⑤ 1 ＿＿＿＿＿＿＿＿＿＿＿＿＿＿＿＿＿＿＿＿＿＿＿＿＿＿＿

2 ＿＿＿＿＿＿＿＿＿＿＿＿＿＿＿＿＿＿＿＿＿＿＿＿＿＿＿

⑥ 1 ＿＿＿＿＿＿＿＿＿＿＿＿＿＿＿＿＿＿＿＿＿＿＿＿＿＿＿

2 ＿＿＿＿＿＿＿＿＿＿＿＿＿＿＿＿＿＿＿＿＿＿＿＿＿＿＿

⑦ 1 ＿＿＿＿＿＿＿＿＿＿＿＿＿＿＿＿＿＿＿＿＿＿＿＿＿＿＿

2 ＿＿＿＿＿＿＿＿＿＿＿＿＿＿＿＿＿＿＿＿＿＿＿＿＿＿＿

⑧ 1 ＿＿＿＿＿＿＿＿＿＿＿＿＿＿＿＿＿＿＿＿＿＿＿＿＿＿＿

2 ＿＿＿＿＿＿＿＿＿＿＿＿＿＿＿＿＿＿＿＿＿＿＿＿＿＿＿

^{*1}ネックレス　necklace

木村さんは　けいたいでんわが　あります。
きむら

KEY SENTENCES

1. 木村さんは　けいたいでんわが　あります。
きむら

2. バードくんは　きょうだいが　二人　あります。
ふたり

3. おとうさんは　きょう　じかんが　ありません。

V O C A B U L A R Y

けいたい（でんわ）	mobile phone (See NOTE)
あります（ある）	have

N E W　K A N J I

雨　　何　　時　　分　　半

 NOTE　Like the English "mobile," けいたい is usually used on its own to mean けいたいでんわ or "mobile phone."

EXERCISES **I**

ex. ボール

ex.	①	②	③

EXERCISES **II**

1. ex. 1　バードくんは　じてん車が　あります。

　　ex. 2　かとうくんは　けいたいでんわが　ありません。

2. ex. 1　A：　バードくんは　じてん車が　ありますか。

　　　　　　B：　はい、あります。

　　ex. 2　A：　かとうくんは　けいたいでんわが　ありますか。

　　　　　　B：　いいえ、ありません。

ex.1	ex.2	①
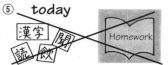		
② older brother	③ sibling	④ friends
⑤ today Homework	⑥ time	⑦ tomorrow appointment

1. ex. バードくんの　おとうさんは　車が　二だい　あります。

2. ex. A：バードくんの　おとうさんは　車が　ありますか。

B：はい、あります。

A：何だい　ありますか。

B：二だい　あります。

ex.

①

②

③

④

sibling

⑤

☆ V O C A B U L A R Y ☆

ボール	ball
お金	money
きっぷ	ticket
やくそく	promise
何だい	how many (cars)
〜だい	(counter for machines, vehicles, etc.)
かぶき	kabuki theater

MAIN DIALOGUE

Yamamoto-kun's mother asks Bādo-kun some questions about his family.

山本くんの　おかあさん：バードくんは　ごきょうだいが
　　　　　　　　　　　　　ありますか。

バードくん　　　　　　　：はい、あねと　おとうとが　あります。

山本くんの　おかあさん：おねえさんは　中学生ですか、こうこう生
　　　　　　　　　　　　　ですか。

バードくん　　　　　　　：十二年生ですから、こうこう　三年生です。

　　　　　　　　　　　　　おとうとは　小学校　四年生です。

☺ バードくんは　おねえさんと　おとうとさんが　あります。

　おねえさんは　こうこう　三年生です。そして　おとうとさんは

　小学校　四年生です。

VOCABULARY

こうこう生	high school student
こうこう	high school
小学校	elementary school

JAPAN NEWS

The Japanese education system, which includes nine years of compulsory education in elementary and junior high school, is shown in the chart below. The school year begins in April and ends in March of the next year.

Kindergarten is optional for children aged three to six years old. All children from six to twelve years of age receive a compulsory elementary education. The remaining three years of the nine-year compulsory education consist of junior high school education.

There are full-time, part-time, and correspondence high schools. In addition to regular courses, some schools offer more vocational studies such as industrial or agricultural sciences. Some 96.7% of junior high school graduates go on to senior high school.

45.2% of senior high school graduates go on to university or junior college (two-year colleges mainly for female students).

SHORT DIALOGUES

1

かとうくんの　おかあさん： 木村さんから　でんわが　ありましたよ。

バードくん　　　　　　　： 何時ごろでしたか。

かとうくんの　おかあさん： 四時すぎでした。

2

かとうくん： あ、雨。　かさが　ない。どうしよう。

　　　　　　バードくん、ある？

バードくん： うん、あるよ。

3

かとうくん： のどが　かわいたね。　お金が　ある？

バードくん： うん、あるよ。

かとうくん： かして。

バードくん： うん、いいよ。

VOCABULARY

雨	rain
ない	don't have (informal speech for ありません)
どうしよう	What shall I do? (informal speech)
ある	have (informal speech for あります)
のどが　かわいた	thirsty (informal speech)
かして	Please lend me (some). (informal speech for かしてください)

学校で　サッカーの　しあいが　あります。
がっ こう

KEY SENTENCES

1. 土よう日に　パーティーが　あります。
   と　　び

2. あした　学校で　テストが　あります。
   がっ こう

3. ぼんおどりって　何ですか。
   なん

☆ VOCABULARY ☆

ぼんおどり	bon dance
～って　何ですか	What is this …? (used when asking about something unfamiliar)
なん	

◆ NEW KANJI ◆

学　　校　　休

EXERCISES Ⅰ

1. ex. はる

ex.
①
②
③

2. ex. ミーティング

ex.
①
②
③

EXERCISES Ⅱ

ex. まいしゅう　かんじの　テストが　あります。

ex. every week

① tonight

② summer

③ next week

④ after match

⑤ last night

⑥ 1998 winter

1. ex. まいしゅう 学校で かんじの テストが あります。
_{がっこう}

2. ex. A: まいしゅう 何が ありますか。
_{なに}

B: かんじの テストが あります。

A: どこで ありますか。

B: 学校で あります。
_{がっこう}

A: いつ ありますか。

B: まいしゅう あります。

ex. every week

① tonight

② summer

③ next week

④ after match

⑤ last night

⑥ 1998 winter

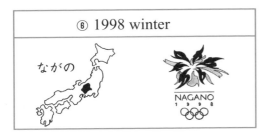

EXERCISES IV

1. ex.　ぼんおどりって　何ですか。
_{なん}

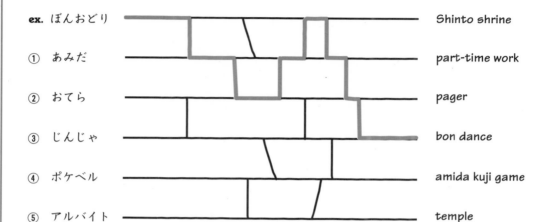

ex. ぼんおどり		Shinto shrine
① あみだ		part-time work
② おてら		pager
③ じんじゃ		bon dance
④ ポケベル		amida kuji game
⑤ アルバイト		temple

2. ex.　入学しきって　何ですか。
_{にゅうがく}　　_{なん}

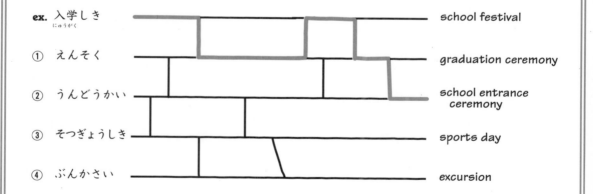

ex. 入学しき		school festival
① えんそく		graduation ceremony
② うんどうかい		school entrance ceremony
③ そつぎょうしき		sports day
④ ぶんかさい		excursion

はる	spring
あき	fall, autumn
ミーティング	meeting
セール	sale
コンサート	concert
オリンピック	Olympics
ながの	Nagano (city and prefecture in central Japan)
あみだ	Amida
じんじゃ	Shinto shrine
ポケベル	beeper, pager
アルバイト	part-time work
入学しき にゅうがく	school entrance ceremony
入学 にゅうがく	entrance to a school
〜しき	ceremony
えんそく	excursion, trip
うんどうかい	sports day, field day
うんどう	sports
〜かい	meet, meeting
そつぎょうしき	graduation ceremony
そつぎょう	graduation
ぶんかさい	school festival
ぶんか	culture

MAIN DIALOGUE

Tanaka-sensē tells Bādo-kun about the bon dancing.

田中先生　：　来月　えきの　前の　こうえんで　ぼんおどりが
　　　　　　　あります。

バードくん：　えっ、ぼんおどりって　何ですか。

田中先生　：　日本の　フォークダンスです。　まいしゅう
　　　　　　　土よう日の　二時から　れんしゅうが　ありますよ。

バードくん：　どこで　ありますか。

田中先生　：　日本中学の　たいいくかんで　あります。

☺　まいしゅう　土よう日の　二時から　日本中学で　ぼんおどりの
　　れんしゅうが　あります。

JAPAN NEWS

The Bon festival is a Buddhist event to hold memorial services for ancestors, from August 13 to 15 in which ancestors' souls are welcomed with sacred fire and seen off with a bonfire for escorting the spirits of the dead. During this period, vegetables and fruit are offered at bon shelves, and in certain regions, people enjoy the bon dance, performed around a drum set on a scaffold.

Companies close down for the festival and many city-dwellers suffer crowded trains or gridlocked highways to make it back to their hometowns in the country. With the New Year holidays, the Bon festival is a rare opportunity for most to visit relatives and friends in the country and so perhaps the mass exodus from Tokyo and resulting traffic is to be expected after all.

VOCABULARY

えっ	What?
フォークダンス	folk dance
まいしゅう	every week
中学／中学校	junior high / junior high school

PREREADING PRACTICE

学校の 一年
<small>がっこう いちねん</small>

四月に 入学しきが あります。
<small>し がつ にゅう がく</small>

四月から 一学きです。
<small>し がつ いち がっ</small>

はるや あきに えんそくや うんどうかいが あります。

七月 二十日ごろから 八月まで 休みます。 なつ休みです。
<small>しち がつ はつか はち がつ やす やす</small>

九月から 二学きです。
<small>く がつ に がっ</small>

あきに ぶんかさいが あります。

十二月 二十五日ごろから 一月 七日ごろまで 休みます。ふゆ休みです。
<small>じゅうに がつ にじゅうご にち いち がつ なのか やす やす</small>

一月から 三学きです。
<small>いち がつ さん がっ</small>

三月に そつぎょうしきが あります。
<small>さん がつ</small>

三月 二十日ごろから 三十一日まで 休みます。 はる休みです。
<small>さん がつ はつか さんじゅういちにち やす やす</small>

VOCABULARY

一学き <small>いちがっ</small>	first semester
～学き <small>がっ</small>	semester
休みます <small>やす</small>	be on vacation

SHORT DIALOGUES

1

か・とうくん　：あした　サッカーの　しあいが　あるよ。

バードくん　：どこで。

かとうくん　：とうきょうこうこうで。

バードくん　：かとうくんは　行く？

かとうくん　：うん、行くよ。

バードくん　：じゃあ、ぼくも　行く。

2

田中先生　　：来しゅう　日本ごの　テストが　あります。
た なかせんせい　　らい　　　にほん

バードくん　：またですか。　いつですか。

田中先生　　：火よう日の　二じかん目です。
た なかせんせい　　か　　び　　に　　め

バードくん　：何かまでですか。
　　　　　　　なん

田中先生　　：二十三かまでです。
た なかせんせい　　に じゅうさん

VOCABULARY

またですか	Again?
二じかん目	second period
〜じかん目	period
二十三か	Lesson 23
〜か	lesson

T A S K ⑮

みそしるって　何ですか。
<small>なん</small>

A is presented with the menu below that lists a number of traditional Japanese dishes. Unsure of what exactly each dish may be, A then asks B to explain using the pattern, 「～って　何ですか」. B then reads out the explanation given below and A writes the names of each dish under the most appropriate picture.

ex.　A：　<u>みそしる</u>って　何ですか。
<small>なん</small>

　　　　B：　Miso soup.

① thin-sliced raw fish
② bowl of rice, topped with tempura and seasoned with a special sauce
③ roll of sushi covered with nori <small>(wafer of dried seaweed)</small>
④ a lacquer box of rice, topped with seasoned eel
⑤ rice ball sometimes covered with nori <small>(wafer of dried seaweed)</small>
⑥ barbecued chicken skewer
⑦ bowl of rice, topped with a pork cutlet
⑧ soup noodle, topped with deep-fried bean-curd

ex. みそしる

1

2

3

4

5

6

7

8

Lesson 25 AN INVITATION

みんなで おはなみを しませんか。

KEY SENTENCES

1. しゅうまつに えいがを 見ませんか。

2. どこで あいましょうか。

3. えきの 前で あいましょう。

VOCABULARY

見ませんか	Would you like to watch [with me] …?
～ませんか	Would you like to … [with me]?
あいましょうか	… shall we meet?
～ましょうか	Shall we …?
あいましょう	[Yes,] let's meet at ….
～ましょう	[Yes,] let's …

NEW KANJI

口 目 耳 手 足

EXERCISES I

ex. 入口
いりぐち

ex.

①

②

③

④

EXERCISES II

ex. たちましょう。

ex.

①

②

③

④

1. **ex.** バードくん　　　　　　　　　：いっしょに　おべんとうを　食べませんか。

　　　かとうくんの　おかあさん：ええ、食べましょう。

ex.

①

②

③

2. ex. かとうくんの　おかあさん：　日よう日に、いっしょに　びじゅつかんへ
　　　　　　　　　　　　　　　　　　　いきませんか。

　　　　　バードくん　　　　　　　：　すみませんが、ちょっと……。

ex.

①

②

③

1. **ex.**　バードくん　　　　　　　　　：　何を　食べましょうか。

　　　かとうくんの　おかあさん：　ハンバーガーを　食べませんか。

　　　バードくん　　　　　　　　　：　ええ、そう　しましょう。

ex.

①

②

③

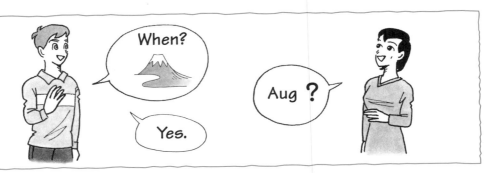

2. ex. バードくん : 何時に あいましょうか。
　　　　かとうくんの　おかあさん : 七時に あいませんか。
　　　　バードくん : 七時は ちょっと……。

ex.

1. **ex.** バードくん　　　　　　　　：何で　行きましょうか。

　　　かとうくんの　おかあさん：バスは　どうですか。

　　　バードくん　　　　　　　　：ええ、いいですね。

ex.

①

②

2. **ex.** バードくん　　　　　　　　　：　何よう日に　パーティーを　しましょうか。

かとうくんの　おかあさん：　金よう日は　どうですか。

バードくん　　　　　　　　　：　金よう日は　ちょっと……。

ex.

①

②

ex. バードくん　： ひるごはんを　食べませんか。

田中先生　： ええ、食べましょう。

バードくん　： 何を　食べましょうか。

田中先生　： サンドイッチを　食べませんか。

バードくん　： いいですね。そう　しましょう。

ex.

①

入口 いりぐち	entrance
出口 でぐち	exit
びじゅつかん	art gallery/museum
えいがかん	movie theater, cinema
たちます（たつ）	stand up
すわります（すわる）	sit down
いっしょに	together, with someone
すみませんが、ちょっと……	I'm afraid that …, I am sorry, but …
ちょっと……	(See NOTE)
スキー	skiing
そう　しましょう	[Yes,] let's do that.

 ちょっと has many surprising uses. It can be used with a hesitant tone to politely decline an invitation to do something with the impression of reluctance.

MAIN DIALOGUE

Bādo-kun suggests a party under the cherry blossoms.

バードくん : 土よう日に みんなで おはなみを
                    しませんか。

山本くんの おかあさん : いいですね。 そう しましょう。
                    どこに 行きましょうか。

バードくん : えきの 前の こうえんは どうですか。

山本くんの おかあさん : ああ、あの こうえんは ほんとうに
                    きれいですね。 何時ごろ 行きましょうか。

バードくん : 十一時ごろ 行きませんか。

山本くんの おかあさん : そうですね。 じゃあ、こうえんで
                    おべんとうを 食べましょう。

☺ バードくんは 土よう日に 山本くんの おかあさんたちと

えきの 前の こうえんで おはなみを します。

JAPAN NEWS

The Japanese have had an affection for cherry blossoms, the national flower, from ancient times. Cherry trees sent to Washington D.C. in 1909 as a token of U.S.-Japan friendship still bloom beautifully every year. People enjoy outdoor parties under the cherry blossoms in the spring. They sit on mats under the cherry trees, eating, drinking, singing cheerfully and viewing the beautiful blossoms.

VOCABULARY

みんなで	all together
（お）はなみを します	view cherry blossoms
（（お）はなみを する)	
（お）はなみ	cherry blossom-viewing
ああ	yes (used to express recognition when someone points out something that you hadn't realized)
あの	(See NOTE)
ほんとうに	really

 This isn't the same あの that you learned in the first Student Book and was used to refer to an object that is located at a distance from both speaker and listener. This あの is used to refer to something with which both speaker and listener are familiar. Note that when both know what is being talked about, an expression such as その　こうえん is never used.

SHORT DIALOGUES

1

田中先生 : じゃあ、ゲームを しましょう。
じゃんけんを しましょう。

バードくんと 山本くん : じゃんけんぽん。 あいこでしょ。

山本くん : かちました。

田中先生 : じゃあ、山本くんの グループから
はじめましょう。

2

かとうくんの おかあさん : みどりの たんじょう日に 何を
あげましょうか。

バードくん : マフラーを あげませんか。

かとうくんの おかあさん : いいですね。

かとうくん : 手ぶくろは どう。

かとうくんの おかあさん : じゃあ、りょうほう あげましょう。

JAPAN NEWS

Janken is the children's game of "paper-scissors-stone," one of many *ken* or fist games that exist in Japan. Players call "jan, ken, pon" and make one of three forms with one hand: stone (closed fist), scissors (two fingers extended), or paper (hand opened flat). Stone "breaks" scissors, scissors "cut" paper, and paper "wraps" stone. If the players happen to make the same fist form then they shout "aiko desho" and start over again. *Janken* is often played to determine who shall be "it" in games of tag or who shall go first in teams.

 グー
いし　stone

 チョキ
はさみ　scissors

 パー
かみ　paper

VOCABULARY

じゃんけんを します（じゃんけんを する）	play the "paper-scissors-stone" game
じゃんけん	"paper-scissors-stone" game
じゃんけんぽん	(See JAPAN NEWS above)
あいこでしょ	(See JAPAN NEWS above)
かちます（かつ）	win
グループ	group
はじめます（はじめる）	start
マフラー	scarf
手ぶくろ	glove, pair of gloves
りょうほう	both

TASK ⑯

なつ休みに　りょこうを　しませんか。
やす

Study the holiday brochures below and then, using the following dialogue as an example, plan an exciting summer vacation with a friend. Write a summary of your holiday plan in the space provided. Note that not all the new vocabulary items are presented as such on these pages. Some of the katakana words originally come from English and so you should be able to guess exactly what they mean. In case you can't, we have included their English equivalents at the foot of the page. As these are just clues, they do not appear in the same order as they do in this task. Good luck!

ハワイ	アフリカ	ヨーロッパ	オーストラリア
7/6–7/13	6/20–7/10	7/5–7/15	7/27–8/13
8/1–8/8	7/7–7/14	8/9–8/27	8/24–9/5
マラソン	サファリ	びじゅつ	スキューバダイビング
サーフィン	ピラミッド	おんがく	サイクリング
ホテル*1	テント	ホテル	ホテル
ユースホステル*2	車 くるま	ユースホステル	友だちの　うち とも

*1ホテル　　　　　　　　　　　　　　hotel
*2ユースホステル　　　　　　　　　　youth hostel

safari　　tent　　pyramid　　cycling　　marathon　　scuba diving

ex.

A： なつ休みに　りょこう*¹を　しませんか。

B： いいですね。　どこに　行きましょうか。

A： ハワイに　行きませんか。

B： ええ。いつ　行きましょうか。

A： 七月　二十日から　八月　一日までは　どうですか。

B： ああ、八月は　ちょっと……。

A： じゃあ、七月に　いきましょう。　どこに　とまりましょう*²か。

B： ユースホステルは　どうですか。

A： それは　いいですね。　ハワイで　何を　しましょうか。

B： サーフィン*³を　しませんか。

A： おもしろいですね。　そう　しましょう。

*¹りょこうを　します（りょこうを　する）　make a trip
　りょこう　　　　　　　　　　　　　　　tour, trip
*²〜に　とまります（とまる）　　　　　 to stay at …
*³サーフィン　　　　　　　　　　　　　surfing

ex.

七月　六日に　友だちと　ハワイへ　行きます。ハワイで　ユースホステルに

とまります。そして　サーフィンを　します。七月　十三日に　かえります。

LET'S TRY!

_____

_____

_____

_____

_____

この　かんじが　分かりません。
わ

KEY SENTENCES

1. 田中先生は　コンピューターが　できます。
   た　なか せん せい

2. 先ぱいは　あした　やきゅうが　できますか。
   せん

3. バードくんは　この　かんじが　分かりません。
   わ

★ V O C A B U L A R Y ★

できます（できる）　　　　can, be able to

◆ N E W　K A N J I ◆

見　　読　　聞

EXERCISES I

1. ex. うんてん

ex. 　① 　② 　③

2. ex. けんどう

ex. 　① 　②

③ 　④ 　⑤

EXERCISES II

1. ex.　バードくんは　じゅうどうが　できます。

　　　　　バードくんは　けんどうが　できません。

2. ex.　A:　バードくんは　じゅうどうが　できますか。

　　　　B:　はい、できます。

　　　　A:　けんどうも　できますか。

　　　　B:　いいえ、けんどうは　できません。

EXERCISES III

1. ex. バードくん： えき前の こうえんで サッカーが できますか。
まえ

田中先生 ： いいえ、できません。
た なか せん せい

ex.

①

②

2. ex. バードくん　　　　　　　　　：おかあさんは　あした　かいものが
　　　　　　　　　　　　　　　　　　できますか。

　　かとうくんの　おかあさん：はい、できます。

ex.

①

②

EXERCISES Ⅳ

1. ex. ローマじを 読みます → ローマじの 読みかた

ex.

①

②

③ のりまき

④ おりがみ

how to read   how to write   how to use   how to make   how to fold

2. ex. バードくんは やさしい かんじが 分かります。

バードくんは むずかしい かんじが 分かりません。

3. ex. A: バードくんは やさしい かんじが 分かりますか。

B: はい、分かります。

A: むずかしい かんじも 分かりますか。

B: いいえ、むずかしい かんじは 分かりません。

	○	×
ex.	easy 山 三 木 日	difficult 漢字 聞 読 飲
①	English	French
②	あいうえお	アイウエオ
③	how to write	how to write

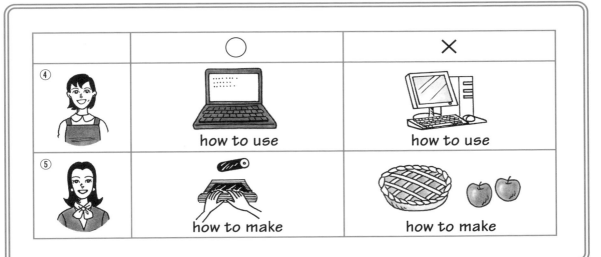

うんてん	driving
ワープロ	word processor
ギター	guitar
ピアノ	piano
けんどう	kendo, Japanese fencing
から手（て）	karate
水えい（すい）	swimming
テニス	tennis
ピンポン	table tennis
ゴルフ	golf
えき前（まえ）	in front of the station
～前（まえ）	in front of …
ローマじ	romanization
読みかた（よ）	how to read
～かた	how to …
つかいます（つかう）	use
のりまき	sushi roll
つくります（つくる）	make
おりがみ	origami
おります（おる）	fold
フランスご	French (language)
レポート	a report
パイ	pie

Bādo-kun asks Tanaka-sensē to show him how to use a word processor.

バードくん ： 先生、ちょっと　いいですか。

田中先生　 ： ええ、いいですよ。　何ですか。

バードくん ： 先生は　ワープロが　できますか。

田中先生　 ： はい、できますよ。

バードくん ： じゃあ、この　ワープロの　つかいかたが
　　　　　　　　分かりますか。

田中先生　 ： ええ、分かりますよ。

バードくん ： すみませんが、おしえてください。

☺ バードくんは　先生に　ワープロの　つかいかたを　聞きました。

VOCABULARY

ちょっと　いいですか	Excuse me, may I ask you something?
ちょっと	excuse me
何ですか	What?
おしえてください	Please show me.
おしえます（おしえる）	show, teach

JAPAN NEWS

Origami is one of Japan's traditional paper crafts. You can make shapes simply by folding a small square of paper. Children are taught how to make origami by their parents or grandparents. Sometimes they learn in kindergarten or preschool. Have a go at making a *tsuru* or crane as shown below.

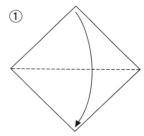

① First fold into a triangle.

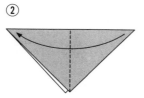

② Fold into a triangle again.

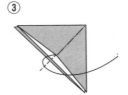

③ Spread open from the inside and fold by pressing down.

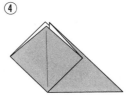

④ Turn over.

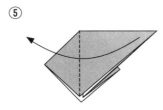

⑤ Swing point to the opposite side.

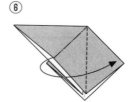

⑥ Spread open from the inside and fold by pressing down.

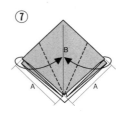

⑦ Align edges A with crease B and fold.

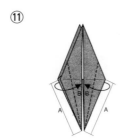

⑧ Press down firmly on the fold before returning to previous position.

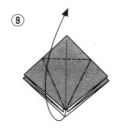

⑨ Spread open from the inside and fold by pressing down, using the creases just made.

⑩ Repeat on reverse.

⑪ Align edges A with center crease B and fold.

⑫ Turn over.

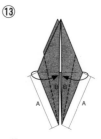

⑬ Repeat on reverse.

⑭

Lift "neck section" at
dotted lines from between
the folds.

⑮

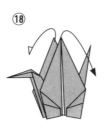

Lift the "neck section"
as shown in the diagram.

⑯

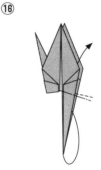

Repeat on opposite side to
make "tail section."

⑰

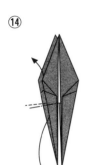

Fold the "neck section" at
dotted lines from between
the folds to make a beak.

⑱

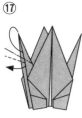

Fold down the wings.

⑲

Here is your complete crane.

JAPAN NEWS

Many words used in Japanese have been borrowed from foreign languages, such as English, French, German, and Dutch. Loanwords are generally written with the katakana script. Since loanwords in full are usually much longer than native Japanese words, there is a tendency to shorten them so that they are easier to pronounce. You have already learned some of these words: テレビ television, スーパー supermarket, and デパート department (store). Sometimes a two-word English phrase is also abbreviated like this: ワープロ word processor. Occasionally, you may come across what seems to be a loanword written in katakana, but the original English word is unrecognizable at first sight. This is because the Japanese often combine two or three English words or a Japanese word with an English word to make a new word that may not exist in English anyway. Do you remember ファミコン from the first book? This word is made up of the English words "family" and "computer" and then abbreviated.

Have a go at the following puzzle. On the left-hand side you will find five such words in katakana and on the right-hand side the original phrases from which they were created. Draw a line to link the katakana word with its correct origin.

① ポケベル•   • radio cassette recorder
② カラオケ•   • remote control
③ リモコン•   • personal computer
④ パソコン•   • empty orchestra
⑤ オフコン•   • pocket bell
⑥ ラジカセ•   • office computer

SHORT DIALOGUES

1

バードくん ： この　もんだいが　分かる？　おしえて。

山本くん　 ： ごめん、ぼくも　分からない。

2

先ぱい　　 ： あした　じゅうどうの　れんしゅうが　できる？

バードくん ： はい、だいじょうぶです。　十時までに　行きます。

3

バードくん ： きのうは　ありがとうございました。

田中先生　 ： レポートは　できましたか。

バードくん ： いいえ、まだです。　あと　二ページです。

VOCABULARY

もんだい	problem
分かる	understand (informal speech for 分かります)
ごめん	sorry (casual for ごめんなさい)
分からない	do not understand (informal speech for 分かりません)
できる	can, be able (informal speech for できます)
十時までに	by 10:00
〜までに	by–
きのうは　ありがとうございました	Thank you for yesterday. (See NOTE)
できましたか	Is [it] finished?
できます（できる）	be ready, be finished, be done
あと	after
二ページ	two pages
〜ページ	(counter for pages)

 It is considered good manners in Japan, as in many other countries, to say thank you to a benefactor who has given you something or done something for you the next time that you meet them.

T A S K ⑰

どんな スポーツが できますか。

I. Choose two sports that you know in Japanese. (The Vocabulary Builder on p. 136 will help you find the Japanese for most sports.) Using the following dialogue as an example, interview three friends to find out if they can do either of the sports that you have chosen. Record the results in the chart provided.

ex.

バードくん： <u>スミスさん</u>は どんな スポーツが できますか。
<u>テニス</u>が できますか。

スミスさん： はい、できます。

バードくん： じゃあ、<u>スキー</u>は どうですか。

スミスさん： <u>スキー</u>も できます。

バードくん： <u>キム[*1]さん</u>は どんな スポーツが できますか。
<u>テニス</u>が できますか。

キムさん ： いいえ、できません。

バードくん： じゃあ、<u>スキー</u>は どうですか。

キムさん ： <u>スキー</u>も できません。

バードくん： <u>ゴメス[*2]くん</u>は どんな スポーツが できますか。
<u>テニス</u>が できますか。

ゴメスくん： はい、できます。

バードくん： じゃあ、<u>スキー</u>は どうですか。

ゴメスくん： <u>スキー</u>は できません。

[*1]キム　Kim (surname)
[*2]ゴメス　Gomez (surname)

		テニス	スキー
ex. スミス	くん／さん	○	○
キム	くん／さん	×	×
ゴメス	くん／さん	○	×
LET'S TRY!		_____	_____
1. _____	くん／さん		
2. _____	くん／さん		
3. _____	くん／さん		

II. Announce the results of your survey as shown in the example below.

ex.

スミスさんは テニスも スキーも できます。

キムさんは テニスも スキーも できません。

ゴメスくんは テニスは できますが、スキーは できません。

LET'S TRY!

_____

_____

_____

Lesson 27

EXPRESSING PREFERENCES

から手と　じゅうどうと　どちらが　好きですか。
　　て　　　　　　　　　　　　　　　　　　　す

KEY SENTENCES

1. バードくんは　車が　好きです。
　　　　　　　　くるま　　す

2. バードくんは　食べものの　中で　ハンバーガーが　いちばん
　　　　　　　　た　　　　　なか
好きです。
す

3. A: バードくんは　じゅうどうと　やきゅうと　どちらが
　　　　じょうずですか。

　　B: やきゅうの　ほうが　じょうずです。

～の　中で なか	of all, among
いちばん	best
どちら	which
～と～と	(particle used for making comparisons)
じょうず（な）	good at, skilful （ーな adj.）(See NOTE)
～の　ほうが	more ...

NEW KANJI

多　少　好　車

The Japanese word じょうずな is used quite differently from its English translations. Take care not to use it when talking about your own abilities—no matter how skilled you may be—or when directly asking someone if they are good at something. It is rarely used in these circumstances. You will learn other expressions to cover these meanings later. じょうずな is normally only used when talking about a third person.

EXERCISES I

1. ex. にんじん

2. ex. スピーチ

EXERCISES II III

II

1. ex. バードくんは　ハンバーガーが　たいへん　好きです。

バードくんは　さしみが　あまり　好きではありません。

2. ex. A：バードくんは　何が　好きですか。

B：ハンバーガーが　好きです。

III

1. ex. バードくんは　スピーチが　たいへん　じょうずです。

バードくんは　さくぶんが　あまり　じょうずではありません。

2. ex. A：バードくんは　何が　じょうずですか。

B：スピーチが　じょうずです。

3. ex. バードくんは　スピーチは　たいへん　じょうずですが、さくぶんは
あまり　じょうずではありません。

	II		III	
	very much	not very much	very	not very
ex.				
①				
②				
③				
④				
⑤				
⑥				

EXERCISES **IV**

1. ex. バードくんは がっきの 中で ピアノが いちばん じょうずです。

2. ex. A: バードくんは がっきの 中で 何が いちばん じょうずですか。

B: ピアノが いちばん じょうずです。

ex.

good at

①

like

②

like

③

good at

④

like

⑤

good at

⑥

like

⑦

like

⑧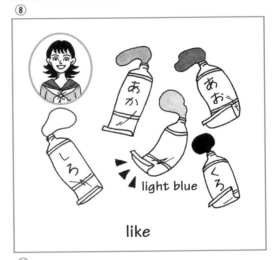

light blue

like

⑨

like

⑩

like

EXERCISES V

ex. バードくん： すしと　てんぷらと　どちらが　好きですか。

　　田中先生　： てんぷらの　ほうが　好きです。
　　た　なか せん せい

ex.

①

②

③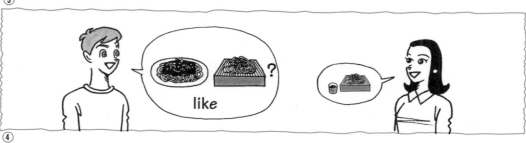

④

V O C A B U L A R Y

にんじん	carrot
たまねぎ	onion
きゅうり	cucumber
さしみ	raw fish
すし	sushi
そば	soba, buckwheat noodles
りょうり	dish, food
スピーチ	speech
さくぶん	composition
うた	song
がっき	musical instrument
せんたく	washing, laundry
きせつ	season
いろ	color
水いろ	light blue
一しゅうかん	one week
～しゅうかん	(counter for weeks)
スケート	skating
スパゲッティ	spaghetti
バイオリン	violin
フルート	flute

VOCABULARY BUILDER 2 Colors

color	いろ	orange	オレンジ（いろ）
black	くろ	pink	ピンク／ももいろ
blue	あお	purple	むらさき（いろ）
brown	ちゃいろ	red	あか
green	みどり	white	しろ
light blue	水いろ	yellow	きいろ
light green	きみどり（いろ）		

*previously learned vocabulary

MAIN DIALOGUE

Tanaka-sensē asks Bādo-kun about his favorite sports.

田中先生 : バードくんは どんな スポーツが 好きですか。

バードくん： じゅうどうや やきゅうが 好きです。

田中先生 : そう。 じゅうどうと やきゅうと どちらが
　　　　　　 好きですか。

バードくん： じゅうどうの ほうが 好きです。
　　　　　　 でも、あまり じょうずではありません。

☺ バードくんは じゅうどうや やきゅうが 好きですが、

　　じゅうどうは あまり じょうずではありません。

JAPAN NEWS

All kinds of sports, including traditional martial arts such as karate, judo, kendo, and sumo, are enjoyed at both professional and amateur level in Japan. The nation's most popular sport is without doubt baseball. As well as the two professional baseball leagues, Central League and Pacific League, amateur high-school baseball can now be said to be a national institution in Japan. Twice annually baseball teams from approximately 4,000 high schools take part in a national knockout competition that is broadcast live on television. Naturally, people support local schools from the region where they grew up.

VOCABULARY

でも	but

VOCABULARY BUILDER 3 — Vegetables

vegetable	*やさい
cabbage	キャベツ
carrot	にんじん
cucumber	きゅうり
lettuce	レタス
onion	*たまねぎ
potato	じゃがいも
spinach	ほうれんそう
sweet potato	さつまいも
tomato	*トマト

VOCABULARY BUILDER 4 — Fruits

fruit	*くだもの	peach	もも
apple	*りんご	persimmon	かき
banana	*バナナ	pineapple	パイナップル
cherry	さくらんぼ	satsuma, mandarin orange	*みかん
grapes	*ぶどう	strawberry	いちご
lemon	レモン	water melon	*すいか
melon	*メロン		

VOCABULARY BUILDER 5 — Sport

sport	*スポーツ	marathon	マラソン
baseball	*やきゅう	rugby	ラグビー
basketball	バスケット（ボール）	scuba diving	スキューバ　ダイビング
cycling	サイクリング	skiing	*スキー
golf	*ゴルフ	soccer	*サッカー
ice skating	*スケート	surfing	*サーフィン
judo	*じゅうどう	table tennis	*ピンポン／たっきゅう
karate	からて	tennis	*テニス
kendo	*けんどう		

VOCABULARY BUILDER 6 — Musical Instruments

musical instrument	*がっき
drum	ドラム
piano	*ピアノ
violin	*バイオリン
flute	*フルート
guitar	*ギター
clarinet	クラリネット
trumpet	トランペット

*previously learned vocabulary

SHORT DIALOGUES

1

木村さん　　　　：から手と　けんどうと　どっちが　好き。

バードくん　　　：けんどうの　ほうが　好き。　でも　へた。

2

バードくん　　　：みどりちゃん、この　中で　どれが　いちばん　好き。

みどりちゃん：これが　いちばん　好き。

バードくん　　　：じゃ、これを　あげるよ。

みどりちゃん：ほんとう、うれしい。

　　　　　　　　　　バードくんが　大好き。

3

かとうくんの　おとうさん：日本の　学校と　アメリカの　学校と　どっち
　　　　　　　　　　　　　　　　　が　好き。

バードくん　　　　　　　　　　　　：うーん、むずかしい　しつもんですね。

　　　　　　　　　　　　　　　　　日本の　学校は　しゅくだいが　多いです。

かとうくんの　おとうさん：アメリカは　少ない？

バードくん　　　　　　　　　　　　：はい、少ないです。

VOCABULARY

どっち	which (more informal than どちら)
へた（な）	poor at (－な adj.)
ほんとう	really
うれしい	happy, pleased, glad
大好き（な）	like very much (－な adj.)
うーん	Umm (used to express hesitation when about to answer something)
しつもん	question
多い	many, much, lots of (－い adj.)
少ない	few, not much (－い adj.)

T A S K ⑱

くろい くつと しろい くつと どちらが かるいですか。

A goes shopping where B is the sales clerk. A asks B questions that compare the various things on sale and B answers. A uses this information to decide what to buy.

ex.

A: <u>くろい くつ</u>と <u>しろい くつ</u>と どちらが <u>かるい</u>*¹ですか。

B: <u>しろい くつ</u>の ほうが <u>かるいです</u>。

A: どちらが <u>じょうぶ</u>*²ですか。

B: <u>りょうほう じょうぶです</u>。

A: どちらが <u>やすいですか</u>。

B: <u>おなじ</u>*³です。

A: じゃあ、<u>しろい くつ</u>を ください。

LET'S SHOP!

*¹かるい   light, not heavy (－い adj.)
*²じょうぶ（な）   strong, durable (－な adj.)
*³おなじ   the same

1.

2.

3.

 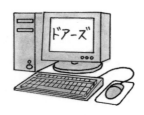

REFERENCE

四かくい   square (－い adj.)
まるい   round (－い adj.)
ことば   word

Lesson 28 SICKNESS

のども　いたいですか。

KEY SENTENCES

1. バードくんは　おなかが　いたいです。

2. （わたしは）　飲みものは　こうちゃが　いいです。

3. バードくんは　あした　サッカーの　しあいが
   ありますから、こんばん　早く　ねます。

VOCABULARY

おなか	stomach
いたい	in pain, hurts, is sore (－い adj.)
こうちゃ	English tea
早く	early

NEW KANJI

食　飲　早

EXERCISES I

ex. あたま

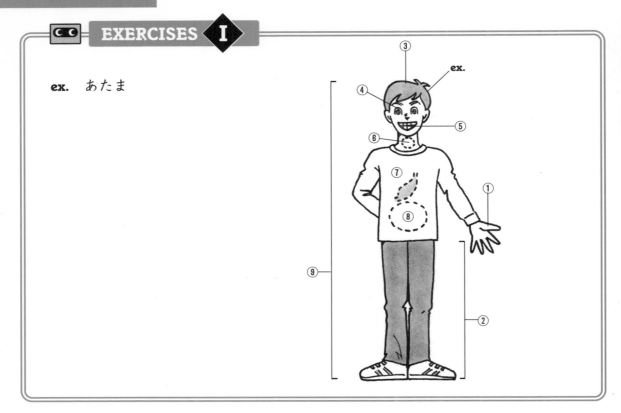

EXERCISES II

ex. みどりちゃんは　目が　大きいです。
め　　　　　おお

ex.

①

②

③

④

⑤

winter

a little

⑥

Japan

1. ex. バードくんは あたまが いたいです。

2. ex. いしゃ ： どう しましたか。

バードくん： あたまが いたいです。

EXERCISES IV

1. ex. 飲みものは　こうちゃが　いいです。

2. ex. A：飲みものは　何が　いいですか。

　　　　B：こうちゃが　いいです。

ex.

①

②

③

④

⑤

committee

1. ex. びょうきですから、学校へ　行きません。

2. ex. A：　どうして　学校へ　行きませんか。

B：　びょうきですから。

ex.

①

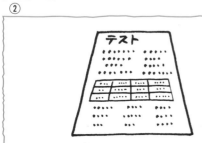
tomorrow

②

tomorrow

③

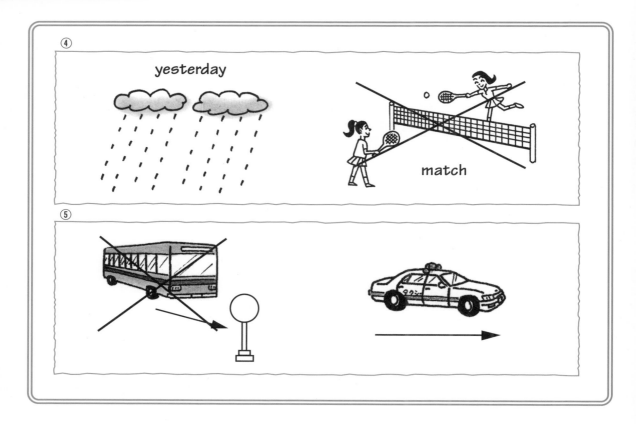

⭐V⭐O⭐C⭐A⭐B⭐U⭐L⭐A⭐R⭐Y⭐

あたま	head
手 て	hand, arm
足 あし	feet, legs
かみ	hair
目 め	eyes
は	teeth
のど	throat
い	stomach
せ	(one's) height
せが　たかい	tall
いしゃ	doctor
どう　しましたか	What is the matter with you?
デザート	dessert
ハワイ	Hawaii
いいん	committee member
どうして	why
カラオケ	karaoke

body	からだ
back	せなか
backside	おしり
chest, breast	むね
ear	耳 みみ
elbow	ひじ
eye	˚目 め
face	かお
finger/toe	ゆび
foot/leg	˚足 あし
hair	˚かみ
hand/arm	˚手 て
head	˚あたま
knee	ひざ
mouth	口 くち
nail	つめ
neck	くび
nose	はな
shoulder	かた
stomach	˚い
stomach	˚おなか
throat	˚のど
tongue	した
tooth	˚は
waist	こし

*previously learned vocabulary

MAIN DIALOGUE

Bādo-kun goes to the hospital.

いしゃ　　　：　どう　しましたか。

バードくん：　おなかが　いたいです。

いしゃ　　　：　ねつが　ありますか。

バードくん：　はい、38ど　あります。

いしゃ　　　：　のども　いたいですか。

バードくん：　はい、少し。

いしゃ　　　：　かぜですね。　くすりを　あげます。　おだいじに。

☺　バードくんは　おなかが　いたいです。ねつが　ありますから、
　　びょういんへ　行きました。　そして　くすりを　もらいました。

★ VOCABULARY ★

ねつ	temperature
38ど	38 degrees Celsius (See NOTE)
〜ど	degree
かぜ	cold
くすり	medicine
おだいじに	I hope you'll get better soon. Please take care of yourself.

 A thermometer for measuring body temperature is an instrument found in most Japanese homes. When people feel ill, they take their own temperature before going to see a doctor. At the hospital too, a nurse will often hand a thermometer to an outpatient while they are waiting to see the physician. 38 degrees Celsius is considerably higher than normal body temperature which is 36.6 degrees Celsius or 98.6 degrees Fahrenheit.

SHORT DIALOGUES

1

田中先生　　：　どうして　しゅくだいを　しませんでしたか。
（たなかせんせい）

バードくん：　あたまが　いたかったですから。

田中先生　　：　そうですか。　もう　だいじょうぶですか。
（たなかせんせい）

バードくん：　はい、ありがとうございます。　だいじょうぶです。

2

木村さん　　：　いつが　つごうが　いい。
（きむら）

バードくん：　土よう日の　ごごが　いい。
　　　　　　　　（ど）（び）

3

バードくん：　デザートは？

木村さん　　：　うん、食べる。
（きむら）　　　　　（た）

バードくん：　飲みものは　何が　いい。コーヒーが　いい、こうちゃが
　　　　　　　（の）　　（なに）
　　　　　　　いい？

木村さん　　：　こうちゃが　いい。
（きむら）

バードくん：　レモン、ミルク？

木村さん　　：　ミルク。
（きむら）

VOCABULARY

つごうが　いい	the best time (lit. Conditions are good.)
つごう	condition, circumstance
レモン	lemon

T A S K ⑲

デザートは 何が いいですか。
なに

First fill in the menu with the katakana words that you know. Now play at waiter and customer with a friend: Ask them what they would like to have. An example dialogue has been printed overleaf.

りょうり	のみもの	デザート
1. _____	1. _____	1. _____
2. _____	2. _____	2. _____
3. _____	3. _____	3. _____
4. _____	4. _____	4. _____
5. _____	5. _____	5. _____

メニュー

ex.

A: りょうりは 何が いいですか。

B: ＿＿＿＿＿＿が いいです。

A: 飲みものは 何が いいですか。

B: ＿＿＿＿＿＿が いいです。

A: デザートは ＿＿＿＿＿＿と ＿＿＿＿＿＿と どちらが いいですか。

B: ＿＿＿＿＿＿が いいです。

Lesson 29

TRANSPORTATION

まいあさ　八ばんの　バスに　のります。
<small>はち</small>

KEY SENTENCES

1. バードくんは　えきで　バスに　のります。

2. おとうさんは　まいあさ　七時半に　うちを　出ます。
<small>しち じ はん</small>　　　　　　　　　<small>で</small>

3. とうきょうから　おおさかまで　しんかんせんで　三じかん
   かかります。
<small>さん</small>

★ V O C A B U L A R Y ★

のります（のる）	get on, ride
出ます（出る） <small>で　　で</small>	go out, leave
おおさか	Osaka (city and prefecture)
三じかん <small>さん</small>	three hours
〜じかん	–hours (counter for hours)
かかります（かかる）	take

◆ N E W　K A N J I ◆

行　　来　　入　　出

EXERCISES I

1. ex.　バスに　のります。
　　　　バスを　おります。

ex.

①
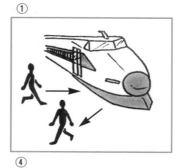

②

③

④
classroom

⑤
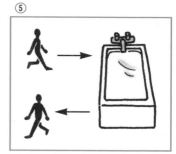

2. ex.　しんじゅくで　バスに　のります。
　　　　ぎんざで　バスを　おります。

ex.

しんじゅく
ぎんざ

①
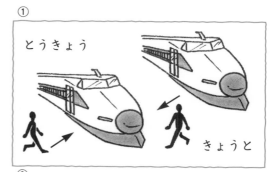
とうきょう
きょうと

②
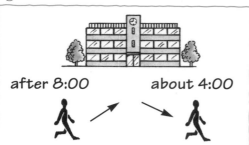
after 8:00　　about 4:00

③

before 9:00　　about 6:30

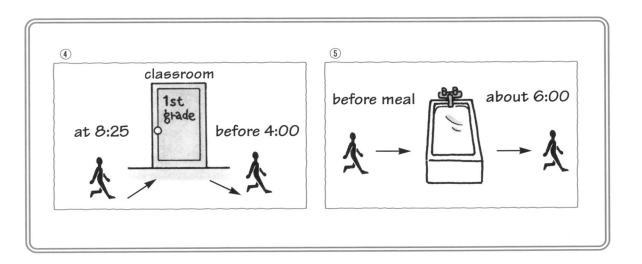

④ classroom 1st grade at 8:25 before 4:00

⑤ before meal about 6:00

PERIODS OF TIME: Minutes

いっぷん（かん）	一分（かん）	1 minute
にふん（かん）	二分（かん）	2 minutes
さんぷん（かん）	三分（かん）	3 minutes
よんぷん（かん）	四分（かん）	4 minutes
ごふん（かん）	五分（かん）	5 minutes
ろっぷん（かん）	六分（かん）	6 minutes
ななふん（かん）	七分（かん）	7 minutes
はっぷん（かん）	八分（かん）	8 minutes
きゅうふん（かん）	九分（かん）	9 minutes
じゅっぷん（かん）	十分（かん）	10 minutes
じゅういっぷん（かん）	十一分（かん）	11 minutes
じゅうにふん（かん）	十二分（かん）	12 minutes
なんぷん（かん）	何分（かん）	how many minutes

EXERCISES II

1. ex.　三じかん　かかります。
　　　　さん

2. ex.　しんかんせんで　三じかん　かかります。
　　　　　　　　　　　さん

3. ex.　とうきょうから　おおさかまで　しんかんせんで　三じかん　かかります。
　　　　　　　　　　　　　　　　　　　　　　　　　　　　さん

4. ex.　A：とうきょうから　おおさかまで　しんかんせんで　どのくらい
　　　　　　かかりますか。

　　　　B：三じかん　かかります。
　　　　　　さん

PERIODS OF TIME: Hours

いちじかん	一じかん	1 hour
にじかん	二じかん	2 hours
さんじかん	三じかん	3 hours
よじかん	四じかん	4 hours
ごじかん	五じかん	5 hours
ろくじかん	六じかん	6 hours
しちじかん	七じかん	7 hours
はちじかん	八じかん	8 hours
くじかん	九じかん	9 hours
じゅうじかん	十じかん	10 hours
じゅういちじかん	十一じかん	11 hours
じゅうにじかん	十二じかん	12 hours
なんじかん	何じかん	how many hours

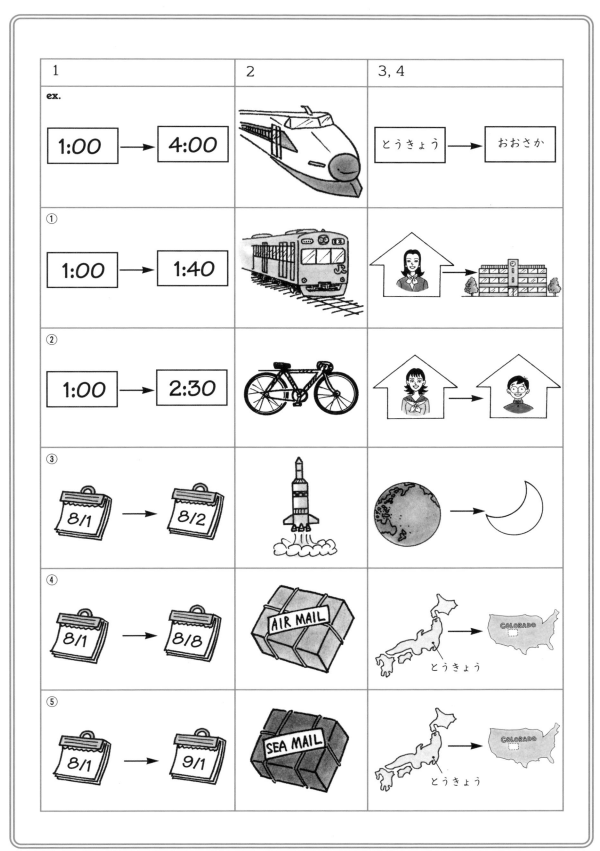

EXERCISES III

ex. どうやって　学校へ　来ますか。
　　　　　　　　がっ こう　　き

ex.  ① ②  ③  ④

VOCABULARY

おります（おりる）	get off
つきます（つく）	arrive
入ります（入る） はい　　はい	enter
（お）ふろ	bath
どのくらい	how long
ロケット	rocket
ちきゅう	earth
月 つき	moon
こうくうびん	air mail
ふなびん	sea mail
どうやって	how

いちにち	一日	1 day
ふつか（かん）	二日（かん）	2 days
みっか（かん）	三日（かん）	3 days
よっか（かん）	四日（かん）	4 days
いつか（かん）	五日（かん）	5 days
むいか（かん）	六日（かん）	6 days
なのか（かん）	七日（かん）	7 days
ようか（かん）	八日（かん）	8 days
ここのか（かん）	九日（かん）	9 days
とおか（かん）	十日（かん）	10 days
じゅういちにち（かん）	十一日（かん）	11 days
じゅうににち（かん）	十二日（かん）	12 days
なんにち（かん）	何日（かん）	how many days

いっしゅうかん	一しゅうかん	1 week
にしゅうかん	二しゅうかん	2 weeks
さんしゅうかん	三しゅうかん	3 weeks
よんしゅうかん	四しゅうかん	4 weeks
ごしゅうかん	五しゅうかん	5 weeks
ろくしゅうかん	六しゅうかん	6 weeks
ななしゅうかん	七しゅうかん	7 weeks
はっしゅうかん	八しゅうかん	8 weeks
きゅうしゅうかん	九しゅうかん	9 weeks
じゅっしゅうかん	十しゅうかん	10 weeks
じゅういっしゅうかん	十一しゅうかん	11 weeks
じゅうにしゅうかん	十二しゅうかん	12 weeks
なんしゅうかん	何しゅうかん	how many weeks

MAIN DIALOGUE

Tanaka-sensē asks Bādo-kun how he gets to school.

田中先生　：　まい日　どうやって　学校へ　来ますか。
たなかせんせい　　　　にち　　　　　　　　　がっこう　き

バードくん：　うちから　えきまで　じてん車に　のります。えき
　　　　　　　で　八ばんの　バスに　のります。　そして　こう
　　　　　　　はち
　　　　　　　えん前で　おります。そこから　あるいて　来ます。
　　　　　　　まえ　　　　　　　　　　　　　　　　　　　き

田中先生　：　そうですか。　うちから　学校まで　どのくらい
たなかせんせい　　　　　　　　　　　　　がっこう
　　　　　　　かかりますか。

バードくん：　三十分ぐらい　かかります。
　　　　　　　さんじゅっぷん

☺ バードくんは　まい日　学校まで　じてん車と　バスで
　　　　　　　　　　にち　がっこう　　　　　しゃ
　行きます。　うちから　えきまで　じてん車に　のります。
　い　　　　　　　　　　　　　　　　しゃ
　えきで　八ばんの　バスに　のります。
　　　　　はち
　そして　こうえん前で　おります。
　　　　　　　　まえ
　そこから　あるいて　学校へ　行きます。　うちから　学校まで
　　　　　　　　　　がっこう　い　　　　　　　　　　がっこう
　三十分ぐらい　かかります。
　さんじゅっぷん

⭐ VOCABULARY ⭐

あるきます（あるく）	walk

SHORT DIALOGUES

①

バードくん ： 日本中学へ どうやって 行きますか。

田中先生 ： えきで 三ばんの バスに のります。

そして 五つ目の バスていで おります。

②

バードくん： すみません、この でん車は 何時に おおさかに
つきますか。

車しょう ： 十一時二十五分に つきます。

バードくん： 十一時二十五分ですね。 ありがとうございます。

③

バードくん ： アメリカまで どのくらい かかりますか。

ゆうびんきょくの 人： こうくうびんですか、ふなびんですか。

バードくん ： ふなびんで おねがいします。

ゆうびんきょくの 人： そうですね。 一か月ぐらい かかります。

VOCABULARY

五つ目	the fifth
～目	(counter for ordinal numbers)
車しょう	(bus or train) conductor

PERIODS OF TIME: Months

いっかげつ（かん）	一か月（かん）	1 month
にかげつ（かん）	二か月（かん）	2 months
さんかげつ（かん）	三か月（かん）	3 months
よんかげつ（かん）	四か月（かん）	4 months
ごかげつ（かん）	五か月（かん）	5 months
ろっかげつ（かん）	六か月（かん）	6 months
ななかげつ（かん）	七か月（かん）	7 months
はっかげつ（かん）	八か月（かん）	8 months
きゅうかげつ（かん）	九か月（かん）	9 months
じゅっかげつ（かん）	十か月（かん）	10 months
じゅういっかげつ（かん）	十一か月（かん）	11 months
じゅうにかげつ（かん）	十二か月（かん）	12 months
なんかげつ（かん）	何か月（かん）	how many months

PERIODS OF TIME: Years

いちねん（かん）	一年（かん）	1 year
にねん（かん）	二年（かん）	2 years
さんねん（かん）	三年（かん）	3 years
よねん（かん）	四年（かん）	4 years
ごねん（かん）	五年（かん）	5 years
ろくねん（かん）	六年（かん）	6 years
しちねん（かん）	七年（かん）	7 years
はちねん（かん）	八年（かん）	8 years
きゅうねん（かん）	九年（かん）	9 years
じゅうねん（かん）	十年（かん）	10 years
じゅういちねん（かん）	十一年（かん）	11 years
じゅうにねん（かん）	十二年（かん）	12 years
なんねん（かん）	何年（かん）	how many years

まず　かぞくに　ついて　はなします。

Bādo-kun is going to make his first speech in Japanese at a local cross-cultural exchange meeting. He is going to address a large number of adults and children. All of the Kato family have come to hear him.

　　はじめまして。　マイク　バードです。　中学校（ちゅうがっこう）　二年生（にねんせい）です。
きょ年（ねん）の八月（はちがつ）に　アメリカの　コロラドから　日本（にほん）へ　来（き）ました。
いま　かとうさんの　おたくに　います。

　　まず　アメリカの　かぞくに　ついて　はなします。
ちちは　べんごしです。　まい日（にち）　とても　いそがしいです。
日本（にほん）の　かいしゃの　しごとも　します。　ときどき　日本（にほん）へ　来（き）ます。
ははは　うちの　しごとを　します。　りょうりが　じょうずです。
よく　おかしを　つくります。　わたしは　ははの　パイが　大好（だいす）きです。
きょうだいが　二人（ふたり）　あります。　あねは　十七（じゅうなな）さいです。　こうこう
三年生（さんねんせい）です。　来年（らいねん）　大学（だいがく）に　行（い）きますから、たくさん　べんきょうを
します。　おとうとは　十（じゅっ）さいです。　小学校（しょうがっこう）　四年生（よねんせい）です。　ときどき
けんかを　しますが、かわいい　おとうとです。　おとうとの　好（す）きな
スポーツは　から手（て）と　スキーです。

つぎに　コロラドに　ついて　せつめいします。

コロラドは　アメリカの　にしに　あります。　人口は　三百三十三万人

ぐらいです。　きれいな町が　たくさん　あります。　なつに　テニスや

キャンプを　します。　ふゆに　スキーが　できます。　山が　たくさん

あります。　みどりが　多い　ところです。

さいごに　日本の　せいかつに　ついて　少し　はなします。

かとうさんの　ごかぞくも　学校の　友だちも　しんせつです。

日本ごは　むずかしいですが、おもしろいです。　こ年の　七月まで　日本に

います。　どうぞ　よろしく　おねがいします。

★ V O C A B U L A R Y ★

まず	first
はなします（はなす）	talk, speak
しごとを　します（しごとを　する）	work, do a job
大学	university
に	to (particle)
けんかを　します（けんかを　する）	have an argument
けんか	argument
つぎに	next
せつめいします（せつめいする）	explain (See NOTE)
にし	west
人口	population
キャンプを　します（キャンプを　する）	go camping
みどり	green
さいごに	finally

◆ N E W   K A N J I ◆

年　　友　　町　　村

NOTE　Here せつめいを　します could have been used instead of せつめいします. With almost all the verbs that end in します, an を can be added or omitted as desired by the speaker. E.g. べんきょう（を）します and キャンプ（を）します

EXERCISES

ex. まず　ひらがなを　ならいます。
つぎに　かたかなを　ならいます。
さいごに　かんじを　ならいます。

ex.

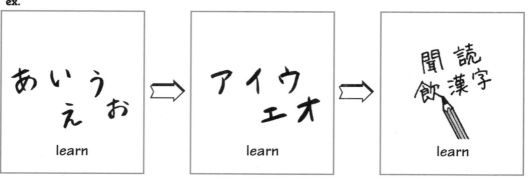

learn　　　　　　learn　　　　　　learn

①

②

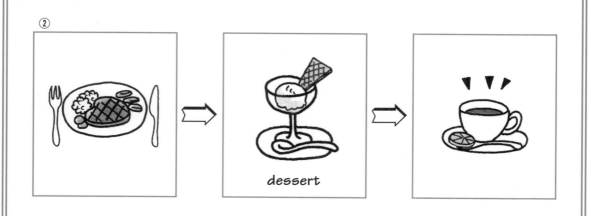

dessert

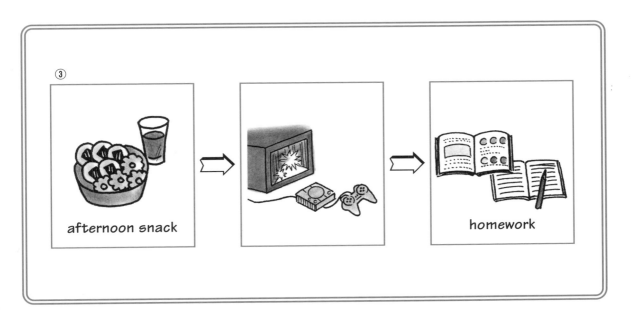

③

afternoon snack

homework

★ V O C A B U L A R Y ★

ならいます（ならう）	learn
あらいます（あらう）	wash
みがきます（みがく）	brush, polish

VOCABULARY BUILDER 8
Occupations

occupation	しごと
accountant	かいけいし
attorney	*べんごし
bank worker	ぎんこういん
civil servant, public employee	こうむいん
corporate employee	*かいしゃいん
doctor	*いしゃ
driver	うんてんしゅ
engineer	エンジニア
nurse	かんごふ
police officer	けいかん
principal	*こうちょう
secretary	ひしょ
teacher	きょうし

*previously learned vocabulary

T A S K ⑳

スピーチを　しましょう。

Write a speech about yourself. Use the following to help you.

はじめまして。＿＿＿＿＿＿＿＿です。　＿＿＿＿＿＿年生です。

ねんせい

＿＿＿＿＿＿＿＿＿＿＿＿＿＿＿＿＿＿＿＿＿＿＿＿＿＿＿＿＿

まず　かぞくに　ついて　はなします。＿＿＿＿＿＿＿＿＿＿＿

＿＿＿＿＿＿＿＿＿＿＿＿＿＿＿＿＿＿＿＿＿＿＿＿＿＿＿＿＿

＿＿＿＿＿＿＿＿＿＿＿＿＿＿＿＿＿＿＿＿＿＿＿＿＿＿＿＿＿

＿＿＿＿＿＿＿＿＿＿＿＿＿＿＿＿＿＿＿＿＿＿＿＿＿＿＿＿＿

きょうだいが　＿＿＿＿＿＿＿＿＿＿＿＿＿＿＿＿＿＿＿＿＿＿

＿＿＿＿＿＿＿＿＿＿＿＿＿＿＿＿＿＿＿＿＿＿＿＿＿＿＿＿＿

＿＿＿＿＿＿＿＿＿＿＿＿＿＿＿＿＿＿＿＿＿＿＿＿＿＿＿＿＿

＿＿＿＿＿＿＿＿＿＿＿＿＿＿＿＿＿＿＿＿＿＿＿＿＿＿＿＿＿

つぎに　わたしの　町に　ついて　せつめいを　します。＿＿＿

まち

人口は　＿＿＿＿＿＿＿＿＿＿＿＿＿＿＿＿＿＿＿＿＿＿＿＿＿

じんこう

さいごに＿＿＿＿＿の　せいかつに　ついて　少し　はなします。＿＿

すこ

＿＿＿＿＿＿＿＿＿＿＿＿＿＿＿＿＿＿＿＿＿＿＿＿＿＿＿＿＿

＿＿＿＿＿＿＿＿＿＿＿＿＿＿＿＿＿＿＿＿＿＿＿＿＿＿＿＿＿

＿＿＿＿＿＿＿＿＿＿＿＿＿＿＿＿＿＿＿＿＿＿＿＿＿＿＿＿＿

どうぞ　よろしく　おねがいします。

REFERENCE

〜に　すんでいます　live in ...

e.g. とうきょうに　すんでいます。

Grammar Review

and

Mini Dictionary
小さいじしょ

Grammar Review

A Sentence Patterns

Sentence patterns	Examples	Lesson
1. ……は ……です	1. ここ<u>は</u> きょうしつ<u>です</u>。	16
	2. がっこう<u>は</u> たのしい<u>です</u>。	19
	3. ともだち<u>は</u> とても しんせつ<u>です</u>。	19
	4. パーティー<u>は</u> たのしかった<u>です</u>。	20
2. ……は ……が ……です	1. わたし<u>は</u> くるま<u>が</u> すき<u>です</u>。	27
	2. バードくん<u>は</u> やきゅう<u>が</u> じょうず<u>です</u>。	27
	3. みどりちゃん<u>は</u> め<u>が</u> おおきい<u>です</u>。	28
	4. バードくん<u>は</u> おなか<u>が</u> いたい<u>です</u>。	28
	5.（わたしは）のみもの<u>は</u> こうちゃ<u>が</u> いい<u>です</u>。	28
3. ……に ……が あります/います	1. いま<u>に</u> テーブル<u>が</u> <u>あります</u>。	17
	2. しょくいんしつ<u>に</u> たなかせんせい<u>が</u> <u>います</u>。	17
4. ……は ……に あります/います	1. でんわ<u>は</u> スーパーのまえ<u>に</u> <u>あります</u>。	18
	2. かとうくん<u>は</u> おてあらい<u>に</u> <u>います</u>。	18
5. ……に ……を ―ます	1. バードくん<u>は</u> おとうさん<u>に</u> てがみ<u>を</u> <u>かきました</u>。	21
	2. きむらさん<u>は</u> バードくん<u>に</u> ノート<u>を</u> <u>あげました</u>。	22
	3. バードくん<u>は</u> きむらさん<u>に</u> ノート<u>を</u> <u>もらいました</u>。	22
6. ……は ……が ―ます	1. きむらさん<u>は</u> けいたいでんわ<u>が</u> <u>あります</u>。	23
	2. たなかせんせい<u>は</u> コンピューター<u>が</u> <u>できます</u>。	26
	3. せんぱい<u>は</u> あした やきゅう<u>が</u> <u>できますか</u>。	26
	4. バードくん<u>は</u> この かんじ<u>が</u> <u>わかりません</u>。	26

Sentence patterns	Examples	Lesson
7. ……で ……が あります	あした がっこう<u>で</u> テスト<u>が</u> <u>あります</u>。	24
8. ……に ―ます	バードくんは えきで バス<u>に</u> <u>のります</u>。	29
9. ……を ―ます	おとうさんは まいあさ しちじ はんに うち<u>を</u> <u>でます</u>。	29
10. ―ませんか	どようびに えいがを <u>みませんか</u>。	25
11. ―ましょうか	どこで <u>あいましょうか</u>。	25
12. ―ましょう	えきの まえで <u>あいましょう</u>。	25

B Interrogatives

Interrogatives	Examples	Lesson
1. なにが	いまに <u>なにが</u> ありますか。	17
	あした がっこうで <u>なにが</u> ありますか。	24
	スポーツの なかで <u>なにが</u> いちばん じょうずですか。	27
なんにん	おんなの ひとが <u>なんにん</u> いますか。	18
なんさつ	ざっしが <u>なんさつ</u> ありますか。	18
なんだい	くるまが <u>なんだい</u> ありますか。	23
なんようびが	いっしゅうかんの なかで <u>なんようびが</u> いちばん すきですか。	27
なにいろが	いろの なかで <u>なにいろが</u> いちばん すきですか。	27
なんじが	ミーティングは <u>なんじが</u> いいですか。	28
2. だれが	にわに <u>だれが</u> いますか。	17
	かぞくの なかで <u>だれが</u> いちばん すきですか。	27
だれに	<u>だれに</u> てがみを かきましたか。	21
	<u>だれに</u> あいますか。	21
3. いつが	きせつの なかで <u>いつが</u> いちばん すきですか。	27
4. どれが	この なかで <u>どれが</u> いちばん すきですか。	27
5. どこ	おてあらいは <u>どこ</u>ですか。	16
どこに	かとうくんは <u>どこに</u> いますか。	17
	ポストは <u>どこに</u> ありますか。	18
	<u>どこに</u> でんわを しましたか。	21
どこで	<u>どこで</u> しあいが ありますか。	24
どこが	アメリカの なかで <u>どこが</u> いちばん すきですか。	27

Sentence patterns	Examples	Lesson
6. どう	べんきょうは <u>どう</u>ですか。	19
	<u>どう</u> しましたか。	28
7. どちら／どっちが	からてと じゅうどうと <u>どちらが</u> すきですか。	27
	やきゅうと サッカーと <u>どっちが</u> すき。	27
8. どうして	<u>どうして</u> がっこうへ いきませんか。	28
9. どのくらい	うちから がっこうまで <u>どのくらい</u> かかりますか。	29
10. どうやって	まいにち <u>どうやって</u> がっこうに きますか。	29

C Verbs & Adjectives

Lesson	Verbs	ー い adjectives	ー な adjectives
17	あります（ある）　be います（いる）　be コピーを　します（する）　make a copy		
19		あかるい　bright おそい　slow かわいい　cute くらい　dark せまい　narrow たかい　high たのしい　enjoyable ちかい　near とおい　far ながい　long はやい　fast ひくい　low, short ひろい　wide ふるい　old みじかい　short むずかしい　difficult やさしい　easy	べんりな　convenient
20		あつい　hot いそがしい　busy さむい　cold	ざんねんな　regrettable だめな　no good にぎやかな　lively ひまな　free
21	あいます（あう）　meet おしえます（おしえる）　tell おねがいします（おねがいする）　please (do) ききます（きく）　ask しつれいします（しつれいする）　be rude ちがいます（ちがう）　be wrong でんわを　します　make a phone call （でんわを　する） びっくりします（びっくりする）　be surprised ファックスを　します（する）　send a fax		
22	あげます（あげる）　give もらいます（もらう）　receive		すきな　liked, favorite すてきな　nice
23	あります（ある）　have のどが　かわきます（かわく）　thirsty		
24	やすみます（やすむ）　be on vacation		

Lesson	Verbs	ー い adjectives	ー な adjectives
25	かちます （かつ）　win じゃんけんを　します （する） 　　play the "stone-scissors-paper" game すわります （すわる）　sit down たちます （たつ）　stand up とまります （とまる）　stay over night はじめます （はじめる）　start はなみを　します （する） see cherry 　　　　　　　　　　　　blossoms りょこうを　します （する）　trip		
26	おしえます （おしえる）　show おります （おりる）　fold できます （できる）　can つくります （つくる）　make つかいます （つかう）　use		
27		うれしい　happy おおい　many, much かるい　light しかくい　square すくない　a little, few まるい　roundt	じょうずな　good at じょうぶな　strong だいすきな　special favorite へたな　poor at
28		いたい　painful, hurts, sore	
29	あるきます （あるく）　walk はいります （はいる）　enter おります （おりる）　get off かかります （かかる）　take でます （でる）　get out つきます （つく）　arrive のります （のる）　get on, ride		
30	あらいます （あらう）　wash キャンプを　します （する）　camp しごとを　します （する）　work すんでいます （すむ）　live せつめいします （せつめいする） 　　　　　　　　　　　　explain ならいます （ならう）　learn はなします （はなす）　talk みがきます （みがく）　brush, polish		

 Note that for verbs two forms are shown. The first is the ー ま す form and the second in parentheses is called the dictionary form. This second form may be said to be the most basic form of a verb and is the one usually listed in dictionaries.

D Particles

Particles	Examples	Lesson
は	1. ひだりの　えでは　へびは　くるまの　うえに　いますが、 　　みぎの　えでは　くるまの　したに　います。	18
	2. Ａ：けんどうも　できますか。	26
	Ｂ：いいえ、けんどうは　できません。	
	3. ジョーンズさんは　テニスは　できますが、スキーは　できません。	26
の	1. つくえの　うえに　コンピューターが　あります。	17
	2. きの　おもちゃを　かいました。	20
	3. せいとの　バードくんです。	21
	4. となりの　おばさんに　もらったの。	22
	5. わたしの　すきな　チームです。	22
	6. おとうさんから　もらうの。	22
	7. レポートの　かきかたが　わかりません。	26
	8. Ａ：コンピューターと　ワープロと　どちらが　べんりですか。	27
	Ｂ：コンピューターの　ほうが　べんりです。	
か	そうですか。	19
から	おとうさんから　もらうの。	22
まで	うちから　がっこうまで　さんじゅっぷん　かかります。	29
までに	じゅうじまでに　いきます。	26
と	からてと　じゅうどうと　どちらが　すきですか。	27
を	1. たなかせんせいを　おねがいします。	21
	2. まいあさ　しちじはんに　うちを　でます。	29

Sentence patterns	Examples	Lesson
も	1. なに<u>も</u>　ありません。	17
	2. だれ<u>も</u>　いません。	17
	3. むずかしい　かんじ<u>も</u>　わかりますか。	26
	4. スミスさんは　テニス<u>も</u>　スキー<u>も</u>　できます。	26
	5. ゴメスくんは　テニス<u>も</u>　スキー<u>も</u>　できません。	26
に	1. いま<u>に</u>　テーブルが　あります。	17
	2. いま<u>に</u>　ねこが　います。	17
	3. ともだち<u>に</u>　あいます。	21
	4. うち<u>に</u>　でんわを　しました。	21
	5. きむらさん<u>に</u>　はなを　あげました。	22
	6. おばあさん<u>に</u>／から　てがみを　もらいました。	22
で	1. ひだりの　え<u>で</u>は　へびは　くるまの　うえに　いますが、みぎの　え<u>で</u>は　くるまの　したに　います。	18
	2. たいいくかん<u>で</u>　じゅうどうの　れんしゅうが　あります。	24
	3. たべものの　なか<u>で</u>　ハンバーガーが　いちばん　すきです。	27
	4. ふなびん<u>で</u>　おねがいします。	29
が	1. にわに　はなや　き<u>が</u>　あります。	17
	2. にわに　いぬ<u>が</u>　います。	17
	3. バードです<u>が</u>、　あきらくんは　いますか。	21
	4. あした　テスト<u>が</u>　あります。	24
	5. A: じゅうどうと　やきゅうと　どちら<u>が</u>　じょうずですか。 B: やきゅうの　ほう<u>が</u>　じょうずです。	27
……は ……が	1. たなかせんせい<u>は</u>　かぶきの　きっぷ<u>が</u>　にまい　あります。	23
	2. たなかせんせい<u>は</u>　コンピューター<u>が</u>　できます。	26
	3. おとうさん<u>は</u>　えいご<u>が</u>　わかります。	26
	4. バードくん<u>は</u>　くるま<u>が</u>　すきです。	27
	5. バードくん<u>は</u>　やきゅう<u>が</u>　じょうずです。	27
	6. にほんの　がっこう<u>は</u>　しゅくだい<u>が</u>　おおいです。	27
	7. みどりちゃん<u>は</u>　め<u>が</u>　おおきいです。	28
	8. バードくん<u>は</u>　おなか<u>が</u>　いたいです。	28
	9. （わたしは）のみもの<u>は</u>　こうちゃ<u>が</u>　いいです。	28

E Adverbs & Adverbial Phrases

Adverbs	Examples	Lesson
いつも	みどりちゃんは　いつも　まんがを　よみます。	10
よく	かとうくんは　よく　ともだちに　でんわを　します。	*21
ときどき	やまもとくんは　ときどき　おんがくを　ききます。	10
あまり	かとうくんは　あまり　てがみを　かきません。	*21
ぜんぜん	おかあさんは　ぜんぜん　スポーツを　しません。	15
もういちど	もういちど　おねがいします。	2
また	では　また　よる　でんわを　します。	21
ちょっと	ちょっと　まってください。	I-Useful Expressions
しょうしょう	しょうしょう　おまちください。	*21
たくさん	テーブルの　うえに　ほんが　たくさん　あります。	18
すこし	かんじは　すこし　むずかしいですが、おもしろいです。	*19
とても	ともだちは　とても　しんせつです。	*19
たいへん	バードくんは　スピーチが　たいへん　じょうずです。	27
いちばん	バードくんは　ハンバーガーが　いちばん　すきです。	27
いま	あきらは　いま　じゅくです。	*21
もう	もう　ひるごはんを　たべましたか。	11
まだ	いいえ、まだです。	*26
あまり	りかは　あまり　むずかしくないです。	20
ぜんぜん	えいがは　ぜんぜん　おもしろくなかったです。	20
いっしょに	いっしょに　おべんとうを　たべませんか。	*25
ぜんぶで	ぜんぶで　いくらですか。	8
ひとりで	バードくんは　ことしの　1がつに　ひとりで　にほんへ　きました。	12
みんなで	みんなで　おはなみを　しませんか。	25
はやく	あした　サッカーの　しあいが　ありますから、こんばん　はやく　ねます。	29
とうとう	バードくんは　とうとう　ゆきこさんに　でんわを　しました。	21
ほんとうに	あの　こうえんは　ほんとうに　きれいですね。	25
まず	まず　ひらがなを　ならいます。	30
つぎに	つぎに　かたかなを　ならいます。	30
さいごに	さいごに　かんじを　ならいます。	30

*Previously learned in the first Student Book.

Mini Dictionary
小さいじしょ

Japanese-English Glossary

日本ご	かんじ	English	Lesson	Page
あ				
ああ		yes (used to express recognition when someone points out something that you hadn't realized)	25	108
あいましょう		[Yes,] let's meet at ….	25	97
あいましょうか		… shall we meet?	25	97
あいます（あう）		meet	21	57
あかるい		bright（－い adj.）	19	39
あき		fall, autumn	24	91
あきら		Akira (given name)	21	64
あげます（あげる）		give	22	69
あし	足	feet, legs	28	144
あそこ		over there	16	1
あたま		head	28	144
あっ		ah	21	66
あつい		hot（－い adj.）	20	52
あと		after	26	124
あのう		Well …, Excuse me, … (used to express hesitation when about to ask or tell someone something)	16	6
あみだ		amida	24	91
あめ	雨	rain	23	86
あらいます（あらう）		wash	30	165
あります（ある）		have	23	81
あります（ある）		is (used for things that cannot move of their own accord, such as books, buildings, plants, vehicles, etc.)	17	9
ある		have (informal speech for あります)	23	86
あるきます（あるく）		walk	29	158
アルバイト		part-time work	24	91
あれっ		Oh!, Oh dear! (used as an exclamation of surprise)	18	23
い				
い		stomach	28	144
E（イー）メール		e-mail	21	63
E（イー）メール　アドレス		e-mail address	21	63
いいん		committee member	28	144
いしゃ		doctor	28	144
いそがしい		busy（－い adj.）	20	52
いたい		in pain, hurts, is sore（－い adj.）	28	139
いちがっき	一学き	first semester	24	94
いちばん		best	27	127
いっしゅうかん	一しゅうかん	one week	27	133
いっしょに		together, with someone	25	107

日本ご	かんじ	English	Lesson	Page
いってください	行ってください	please go	16	6
いぬ	犬	dog	17	13
います（いる）		is (used for living things that move, such as people, animals, etc.)	17	9
いりぐち	入口	entrance	25	107
いろ		color	27	133

う

ううん		no (informal word for いいえ)	17	16
うーん		Umm (used to express hesitation when about to answer something)	27	137
うえ	上	on	17	9
うけつけ		reception	16	5
うしろ		back, behind	17	13
うた		song	27	133
うれしい		happy, pleased, glad	27	137
うんてん		driving	26	119
うんどう		sports	24	91
うんどうかい		sports day, field day	24	91

え

えいがかん		movie theater, cinema	25	107
えきまえ	えき前	in front of the station	26	119
えっ		What?	24	92
えんそく		excursion, trip	24	91

お

おおい	多い	many, much, lots of (－い adj.)	27	137
おおさか		Osaka (city and prefecture)	29	151
おかね	お金	money	23	83
おきなわ		Okinawa (name of island group south of Kyushu)	20	52
おしえてください		Please show me.	26	120
おしえてください		Please tell me.	19	44
おしえます（おしえる）		show, teach	26	120
おしえます（おしえる）		tell	21	63
おじいさん		(someone else's) grandfather	21	63
（お）しょうがつ	（お）正月	New Year's Day	22	78
おそい		slow (－い adj.)	19	39
おたく		(someone else's) home	21	64
おだいじに		I hope you'll get better soon. Please take care of yourself.	28	146
（お）てあらい	（お）手あらい	toilet, lavatory	16	1
おとしだま	お年だま	a New Year's gift	22	75
おなか		stomach	28	139
おなじ		the same	27	138
おばあさん		(someone else's) grandmother	21	63
（お）はなみ		cherry blossom-viewing	25	108
（お）はなみを します（する）		view cherry blossoms	25	108
（お）ふろ		bath	29	15
（お）まつり		festival	20	52
おもちゃ		toy	17	13
おやつ		afternoon snack	18	27
おりがみ		origami	26	119
おります（おりる）		get off	29	156
おります（おる）		fold	26	119
オリンピック		Olympics	24	91

か

～か		lesson	24	95

日本ご	かんじ	English	Lesson	Page
こうこう		high school	23	84
こうこうせい	こうこう生	high school student	23	84
こうちゃ		English tea	28	139
こうちょうしつ		principal's office	16	5
こうてい		school grounds	16	5
こうばん		police box	17	16
ごきょうだい		(someone else's) brothers and sisters	21	63
ここ		here	16	1
ことば		word	27	138
コピー		a copy	17	16
コピーを　します（する）		make a copy	17	16
ゴメス		Gomez (surname)	26	126
ごめん		sorry (casual for ごめんなさい)	26	124
ごりょうしん		(someone else's) parents	21	63
ゴルフ		golf	26	119
コンサート		concert	24	91
コンビニ		convenience store	17	16
コンピューター		computer	16	5
コンピュータールーム		computer room	16	5

さ

さいごに		finally	30	163
さいふ		wallet, purse	18	23
さくぶん		composition	27	133
さしみ		raw fish	27	133
～さつ		(counter for books)	18	23
さむい		cold (－い adj.)	20	52
ざんねん（な）		regrettable (－な adj.)	20	52

し

しあい		competition	20	52
しかくい	四かくい	square (－い adj.)	27	138
じかん		time	18	27
～じかん		–hours (counter for hours)	29	151
～じかんめ	～じかん目	period	24	95
～しき		ceremony	24	91
しごとを　します（する）		work, do a job	30	163
した	下	under	17	13
～しつ		–office	16	5
しつもん		question	27	137
しつれいしました		I'm sorry.	21	66
しつれいします		Goodbye. (lit. I'm going to be rude [and ring off].)		
じゃんけん		"paper-scissors-stone" game	25	110
じゃんけんを　します（する）		play the "paper-scissors-stone" game	25	110
しゃしょう	車しょう	(bus or train) conductor	29	161
～しゅうかん		(counter for weeks)	27	133
じゅうしょ		address	21	63
しゅうまつ		weekend	20	52
じゅく		cram school	21	64
（お）しょうがつ	（お）正月	New Year's Day	22	78
しょうがっこう	小学校	elementary school	23	84
じょうず（な）		good at, skilful　（－な adj.)	27	127
じょうぶ（な）		strong, durable (－な adj.)	27	138
しょくいん		staff	16	5
しょくいんしつ		teachers' lounge, staff room	16	5
しょくどう	食どう	dining room	17	14
じんこう	人口	population	30	163

日本ご	かんじ	English	Lesson	Page
じんじゃ		Shinto shrine	24	91
しんじゅく		Shinjuku (name of area in Tokyo)	16	8

す

日本ご	かんじ	English	Lesson	Page
すいえい	水えい	swimming	26	119
スキー		skiing	25	107
すき（な）	好き（な）	likable, favorite（－い adj.）	22	76
すくない	少ない	few, not much（－い adj.）	27	137
スケート		skating	27	133
すし		sushi	27	133
すてき（な）		nice, fine, wonderful（－な adj.）	22	75
スパゲッティ		spaghetti	27	133
スピーチ		speech	27	133
すみませんが、ちょっと……		I am sorry, but …	25	107
すわります（すわる）		sit down	25	107
すんでいます		live	30	166

せ

日本ご	かんじ	English	Lesson	Page
せ		(one's) height	28	144
セール		sale	19	39
せいふく		school uniform	28	144
せが　たかい		tall	30	163
せつめいします（せつめいする）		explain	19	39
せまい		narrow（－い adj.）	20	45
ぜんぜん…くなかったです。		… (not) at all	20	52
せんせんしゅう		the week before last	20	52
せんたく		washing, laundry	27	133

そ

日本ご	かんじ	English	Lesson	Page
そう　しましょう		[Yes,] let's do that.	25	107
そうですか		I see.	19	42
そこ		there	16	5
そつぎょう		graduation	24	91
そつぎょうしき		graduation ceremony	24	91
そば		soba, buckwheat noodles	27	133
そふ		my grandfather	21	63
ソファー		sofa	17	13
そぼ		my grandmother	21	63
それは　ざんねんでしたね。		That's a pity.	20	52
それは　よかったですね。		That's nice.	20	52

た

日本ご	かんじ	English	Lesson	Page
～だい		(counter for machines, vehicles, etc.)	23	83
だいがく	大学	university	30	163
だいすき（な）	大好き（な）	like very much（－な adj.）	27	137
だいどころ		kitchen	17	14
たかい		high（－い adj.）	19	39
たくさん		many, a lot of	18	17
タクシーのりば		taxi stand, taxi rank	17	13
だけ		only	22	78
～たち		(plural suffix used for people)	22	76
たちます（たつ）		stand up	25	107
たてもの		building	19	39
たのしい		enjoyable（－い adj.）	19	29
たべもの	食べもの	food, things to eat	19	39
たま		Tama (common name for a cat)	22	78
たまねぎ		onion	27	133

日本ご	かんじ	English	Lesson	Page
～まえ	～前	in front of …	26	119
～ましょう		[Yes,] let's …	25	97
～ましょうか		Shall we …?	25	97
まず		first	30	163
～ませんか		Would you like to … [with me]?	25	97
また		again		
またですか		Again?	24	95
まっすぐ		straight on	16	6
～までに		by–	24	123
マフラー		scarf	25	110
まるい		round (－い adj.)	27	138

み

日本ご	かんじ	English	Lesson	Page
ミーティング		meeting	24	91
みがきます（みがく）		brush, polish	30	165
みぎ		right	19	25
みじかい		short (－い adj.)	19	39
みずいろ	水いろ	light blue	27	133
みどり		green	30	163
みなみ		south	16	8
みんな		everybody	18	27
みんなで		all together	25	108

む

日本ご	かんじ	English	Lesson	Page
むずかしい		difficult (－い adj.)	19	29
むずかしくないです		… is not difficult	19	29

め

日本ご	かんじ	English	Lesson	Page
め	目	eyes	28	144
～め	～目	(counter for ordinal numbers)	29	161
めがね		(eye) glasses, spectacles	17	13

も

日本ご	かんじ	English	Lesson	Page
もしもし		hello (chiefly used on the telephone)	21	64
もらいます（もらう）		receive	22	69
もらう		receive (informal for もらいます)	22	78
もらった		received (informal for もらいました)	22	78
もんだい		problem	26	124

や

日本ご	かんじ	English	Lesson	Page
やきゅう		baseball	22	75
やくそく		promise	23	83
やさい		vegetable	17	13
やさしい		easy (－い adj.)	19	39
～やすみ	～休み	vacation, holiday	19	39
やすみます	休みます	be on vacation	24	94

ゆ

日本ご	かんじ	English	Lesson	Page
ユースホステル		youth hostel	25	111
～ゆき	～行き	bound for–	16	8
ゆきこ	ゆき子	Yukiko (given name)	21	68

よ

日本ご	かんじ	English	Lesson	Page
よみかた	読みかた	how to read	26	119
よる		night	21	64

English-Japanese Glossary

English	日本ご	かんじ	Lesson	Page
A				
a lot of	たくさん		18	17
about	〜ぐらい		19	42
about …	〜に ついて		19	44
address	じゅうしょ		21	63
after	あと		26	124
afternoon snack	おやつ		18	27
Again?	またですか		24	95
ah	あっ		21	66
air mail	こうくうびん		29	156
all together	みんなで		25	108
among	〜の なかで	〜の 中で	27	127
argument	けんか		30	163
(have an) argument	けんかを します（する）		30	163
arrive	つきます（つく）		29	156
art gallery/museum	びじゅつかん		25	107
ask	ききます（きく）	聞きます（聞く）	21	63
at last	とうとう		21	68
autumn	あき		24	91
B				
back	うしろ		17	13
ball	ボール		23	83
baseball	やきゅう		22	75
basement	ちか		17	13
basket	かご		18	23
bath	（お）ふろ		29	156
be able to	できます（できる）		26	113
be done	できます（できる）		26	124
be finished	できます（できる）		26	124
be on vacation	やすみます	休みます	24	94
be ready	できます（できる）		26	124
be surprised	びっくりします（する）		21	66
beeper	ポケベル		24	91
beer	ビール		27	133
before	まえ	前	17	13
behind	うしろ		17	13
best	いちばん		27	127
bird	とり		17	13
bon dance	ぼんおどり		24	87
book (counter)	〜さつ		18	23
bookshelf	ほんだな	本だな	17	13
both	りょうほう		25	110
bound for–	〜ゆき	〜行き	16	8
box	はこ		18	23
bright	あかるい		19	39
brothers and sisters (own)	きょうだい		21	63
brothers and sisters (someone else's)	ごきょうだい		21	63
brush	みがきます（みがく）		30	165
buckwheat noodles	そば		27	133

English	日本ご	かんじ	Lesson	Page
in front of	まえ	前	17	13
in front of the station	えきまえ	えき前	26	119
in front of ...	～まえ	～前	26	119
in pain	いたい		28	139
infirmary	ほけんしつ		16	5
inside	なか	中	17	13
is	あります （ある）			
	(used for things that cannot move of their own accord,			
	such as books, buildings, plants, vehicles, etc.);		17	9
	います （いる）			
	(used for living things that move, such as people, animals, etc.)		17	9
	でございます (very polite word for です)		21	66

J

English	日本ご	かんじ	Lesson	Page
Japanese fencing	けんどう		26	119
junior high	ちゅうがく	中学	24	92
junior high school	ちゅうがっこう	中学校	24	92

K

English	日本ご	かんじ	Lesson	Page
kabuki theater	かぶき		23	83
karaoke	カラオケ		28	144
karate	からて	から手	26	119
kendo	けんどう		26	119
kitchen	だいどころ		17	14

L

English	日本ご	かんじ	Lesson	Page
laundry	せんたく		27	133
lavatory	（お）てあらい	（お）手あらい	16	1
learn	ならいます （ならう）		30	165
leave	でます （でる）	出ます （出る）	29	151
left	ひだり		16	5
legs	あし	足	28	144
lemon	レモン		28	148
lesson	～か		24	95
[Yes,] let's meet at ….	あいましょう		25	97
[Yes,] let's do that.	そう しましょう		25	107
[Yes,] let's ...	～ましょう		25	97
letter box	ポスト		18	23
library	としょしつ		16	6
light (not heavy)	かるい		27	128
light blue	みずいろ	水いろ	27	133
likable	すき （な）	好き （な）	22	76
live	すんでいます		30	166
lively	にぎやか （な）		20	52
locker	ロッカー		18	23
locker rooms	こういしつ		16	5
long	ながい		19	39
Look!	ほら (used to get someone's attention)		18	27
lots of	おおい	多い	27	137
low	ひくい		19	39

M

English	日本ご	かんじ	Lesson	Page
machines (counter)	～だい		23	83
mail box	ポスト		18	23
main entrance and exit	ちゅうおうぐち	ちゅうおう口	16	8
make	つくります （つくる）		26	119
make a copy	コピーを します （する）		17	16
make a phone call	でんわを します （する）		21	57

English	日本ご	かんじ	Lesson	Page
parents (someone else's)	ごりょうしん		21	63
parents (own)	りょうしん		21	63
parking lot	ちゅうしゃじょう		17	13
part-time work	アルバイト		24	91
period	～じかんめ	～じかん目	24	95
piano	ピアノ		26	119
pie	パイ		26	119
please go	いってください	行ってください	16	5
Please lend me (some).	かして (informal speech for かしてください)		23	86
Please show me.	おしえてください		26	120
Please tell me	おしえてください		19	44
pleased	うれしい		27	137
police box	こうばん		17	16
polish	みがきます (みがく)		30	165
poor at	へた (な)		27	137
population	じんこう	人口	30	163
present	プレゼント		22	75
principal's office	こうちょうしつ		16	5
problem	もんだい		26	124
promise	やくそく		23	83
purse	さいふ		18	23

Q

| question | しつもん | | 27 | 137 |

R

rain	あめ	雨	23	86
raw fish	さしみ		27	133
really	ほんとう		27	137
really	ほんとうに		25	108
receive	もらいます (もらう)		22	69
received	もらった (informal for もらいました)		22	78
reception	うけつけ		16	5
refrigerator	れいぞうこ		18	27
regrettable	ざんねん (な)		20	52
(a) report	レポート		26	119
ride	のります (のる)		29	151
right	みぎ		17	16
rocket	ロケット		29	156
romanization	ローマじ		26	119
room	ルーム		16	5
round	まるい		27	138

S

(the) same	おなじ		27	138
scarf	マフラー		25	110
school club	クラブ		19	39
school entrance ceremony	にゅうがくしき	入学しき	24	91
school festival	ぶんかさい		24	91
school grounds	こうてい		16	5
school uniform	せいふく		19	39
sea mail	ふなびん		29	156
season	きせつ		27	133
semester	～がっき	～学き	24	94
send a fax	ファックスを します (する)		21	63
... shall we meet?	あいましょうか		25	97
Shall we ...?	～ましょうか		25	97
Shinto shrine	じんじゃ		24	91

English	日本ご	かんじ	Lesson	Page
there	そこ		16	5
things to drink	のみもの	飲みもの	19	39
things to eat	たべもの	食べもの	19	39
thirsty (informal speech)	のどが　かわいた		23	26
throat	のど		28	144
ticket	きっぷ		23	83
ticket gate	かいさつぐち	かいさつ口	16	8
time	じかん		18	27
to	に (indirect object marker, particle)		21	57
to stay at	とまります　（とまる）		25	111
together	いっしょに		25	107
toilet	おてあらい	お手あらい	16	1
tooth	は		28	144
tour	りょこう		25	111
toy	おもちゃ		17	13
transport	のりもの		19	39
tree	き	木	17	13
trip	りょこう		25	111
trip	えんそく		24	91

U

English	日本ご	かんじ	Lesson	Page
Umm	うーん (used to express hesitation when about to answer something)		27	137
under	した	下	17	13
understand	わかる	分かる	26	124
university	だいがく	大学	30	163
use	つかいます　（つかう）		26	119

V

English	日本ご	かんじ	Lesson	Page
vacation	～やすみ	～休み	19	39
vegetable	やさい		17	13
vehicles (counter)	～だい		23	83
very	とっても (more informal than とても)		19	42
view cherry blossoms	（お）はなみを　します	（お）はなみを　する	25	108
violin	バイオリン		27	133

W

English	日本ご	かんじ	Lesson	Page
walk	あるきます　（あるく）		29	158
wallet	さいふ		18	23
wash	あらいます　（あらう）		30	165
washing	せんたく		27	133
week (counter)	～しゅうかん		27	133
week before last	せんせんしゅう		20	52
weekend	しゅうまつ		20	52
west	にし		30	163
What is the matter with you?	どう　しましたか		28	144
What is this …?	～って　なんですか	～って　何ですか	24	87
What shall I do?	どうしよう		23	86
What?	えっ		24	92
which	どちら		27	127
which (informal)	どっち		27	137
why	どうして		28	144
wide	ひろい		19	39
win	かちます　（かつ）		25	110
winter	ふゆ		19	39
with someone	いっしょに		25	107
woman next door	となりの　おばさん		22	78

English	日本ご		かんじ	Lesson	Page
wonderful	すてき （な）			22	75
wood	き		木	20	54
word	ことば			27	138
word processor	ワープロ			26	119
work	しごとを　します（する）			30	163
Would you like to watch [with me] ...?	みませんか		見ませんか	25	97
Would you like to ... [with me]?	〜ませんか			25	97

Y

–year primary pupil	〜ねんせい		〜年生	16	5
–year	〜ねん		〜年	16	5
yes	ああ (used to express recognition when someone points out something that you hadn't realized)			25	108
youth hostel	ユースホステル			25	112

ヤングのための日本語　第2巻　スチューデントブック
JAPANESE FOR YOUNG PEOPLE II　Student Book

1999年 5 月　第 1 刷発行
2003年12月　第 2 刷発行

著 者　社団法人　国際日本語普及協会

発行者　畑野文夫

発行所　講談社インターナショナル株式会社
　　　　〒112-8652 東京都文京区音羽 1-17-14
　　　　電話　03-3944-6493（編集部）
　　　　　　　03-3944-6492（営業部・業務部）
　　　　ホームページ　www.kodansha-intl.co.jp

印刷・製本所　大日本印刷株式会社

JAPANESE LANGUAGE GUIDES

Easy-to-use guides to essential language skills

13 SECRETS FOR SPEAKING FLUENT JAPANESE

日本語をペラペラ話すための13の秘訣　*Giles Murray*

The most fun, rewarding, and universal techniques of successful learners of Japanese that anyone can put immediately to use. A unique and exciting alternative, full of lively commentaries, comical illustrations, and brain-teasing puzzles.

Paperback, 184 pages; ISBN 4-7700-2302-2

ALL ABOUT PARTICLES　新装版 助詞で変わるあなたの日本語　*Naoko Chino*

The most common and less common particles brought together and broken down into some 200 usages, with abundant sample sentences.

Paperback, 160 pages; ISBN 4-7700-2781-8

JAPANESE VERBS AT A GLANCE　新装版 日本語の動詞　*Naoko Chino*

Clear and straightforward explanations of Japanese verbs—their functions, forms, roles, and politeness levels.

Paperback, 180 pages; ISBN 4-7700-2765-6

BEYOND POLITE JAPANESE: A Dictionary of Japanese Slang and Colloquialisms

新装版 役に立つ話しことば辞典　*Akihiko Yonekawa*

Expressions that all Japanese, but few foreigners, know and use every day. Sample sentences for every entry.

Paperback, 176 pages; ISBN 4-7700-2773-7

BUILDING WORD POWER IN JAPANESE: Using Kanji Prefixes and Suffixes

新装版 増えて使えるヴォキャブラリー　*Timothy J. Vance*

Expand vocabulary and improve reading comprehension by modifying your existing lexicon.

Paperback, 128 pages; ISBN 4-7700-2799-0

HOW TO SOUND INTELLIGENT IN JAPANESE: A Vocabulary Builder

新装版 日本語の知的表現　*Charles De Wolf*

Lists, defines, and gives examples for the vocabulary necessary to engage in intelligent conversation in fields such as politics, art, literature, business, and science.

Paperback, 160 pages; ISBN 4-7700-2859-8

MAKING SENSE OF JAPANESE: What the Textbooks Don't Tell You

新装版 日本語の秘訣　*Jay Rubin*

"Brief, wittily written essays that gamely attempt to explain some of the more frustrating hurdles [of Japanese].... They can be read and enjoyed by students at any level."

—*Asahi Evening News*

Paperback, 144 pages; ISBN 4-7700-2802-4

LOVE, HATE and Everything in Between: Expressing Emotions in Japanese

新装版 日本語の感情表現集　*Mamiko Murakami*

Includes more than 400 phrases that are useful when talking about personal experience and nuances of feeling.

Paperback, 176 pages; ISBN 4-7700-2803-2

www.thejapanpage.com

JAPANESE LANGUAGE GUIDES

Easy-to-use guides to essential language skills

THE HANDBOOK OF JAPANESE VERBS　日本語動詞ハンドブック　*Taeko Kamiya*

An indispensable reference and guide to Japanese verbs aimed at beginning and intermediate students. Precisely the book that verb-challenged students have been looking for.

• Verbs are grouped, conjugated, and combined with auxiliaries
• Different forms are used in sentences　• Each form is followed by reinforcing examples and exercises

Paperback, 256 pages; ISBN 4-7700-2683-8

THE HANDBOOK OF JAPANESE ADJECTIVES AND ADVERBS

日本語形容詞・副詞ハンドブック　*Taeko Kamiya*

The ultimate reference manual for those seeking a deeper understanding of Japanese adjectives and adverbs and how they are used in sentences. Ideal, too, for those simply wishing to expand their vocabulary or speak livelier Japanese.

Paperback, 336 pages; ISBN 4-7700-2879-2

A HANDBOOK OF COMMON JAPANESE PHRASES

日本語決まり文句辞典　*Sanseido*

Japanese is rich in common phrases perfect for any number and variety of occasions. This handbook lists some 600 of them and explains when, where, and how to use them, providing alternatives for slightly varied circumstances and revealing their underlying psychology.

Paperback, 320 pages; ISBN 4-7700-2798-2

BASIC CONNECTIONS: Making Your Japanese Flow

新装版 日本語の基礎ルール　*Kakuko Shoji*

Explains how words and phrases dovetail, how clauses pair up with other clauses, how sentences come together to create harmonious paragraphs. The goal is to enable the student to speak both coherently and smoothly.

Paperback, 160 pages; ISBN 4-7700-2860-1

JAPANESE CORE WORDS AND PHRASES: Things You Can't Find in a Dictionary

新装版 辞書では解らない慣用表現　*Kakuko Shoji*

Some Japanese words and phrases, even though they lie at the core of the language, forever elude the student's grasp. This book brings these recalcitrants to bay.

Paperback, 144 pages; ISBN 4-7700-2774-5

READ REAL JAPANESE: All You Need to Enjoy Eight Contemporary Writers

新装版 日本語で読もう　*Janet Ashby*

Original Japanese essays by Yoko Mori, Ryuichi Sakamoto, Machi Tawara, Shoichi Nejime, Momoko Sakura, Seiko Ito, Banana Yoshimoto, and Haruki Murakami. With vocabulary lists giving the English for Japanese words and phrases and also notes on grammar, nuance, and idiomatic usage.

Paperback, 168 pages; ISBN 4-7700-2936-5

BREAKING INTO JAPANESE LITERATURE: Seven Modern Classics in Parallel Text

日本語を読むための七つの物語　*Giles Murray*

Read classics of modern Japanese fiction in the original with the aid of a built-in, customized dictionary, free MP3 sound files of professional Japanese narrators reading the stories, and literal English translations. Features Ryunosuke Akutagawa's "Rashomon" and other stories.

Paperback, 240 pages; ISBN 4-7700-2899-7

www.thejapanpage.com

KODANSHA INTERNATIONAL DICTIONARIES

Easy-to-use dictionaries designed for non-native learners of Japanese.

KODANSHA'S FURIGANA JAPANESE DICTIONARY

JAPANESE-ENGLISH / ENGLISH-JAPANESE ふりがな和英・英和辞典

Both of Kodansha's popular furigana dictionaries in one portable, affordable volume. A truly comprehensive and practical dictionary for English-speaking learners, and an invaluable guide to using the Japanese language.
• 30,000-word basic vocabulary • Hundreds of special words, names, and phrases
• Clear explanations of semantic and usage differences • Special information on grammar and usage
Hardcover, 1318 pages; ISBN 4-7700-2480-0

KODANSHA'S FURIGANA JAPANESE-ENGLISH DICTIONARY

新装版 ふりがな和英辞典

The essential dictionary for all students of Japanese.
• Furigana readings added to all *kanji* • 16,000-word basic vocabulary
Paperback, 592 pages; ISBN 4-7700-2750-8

KODANSHA'S FURIGANA ENGLISH-JAPANESE DICTIONARY

新装版 ふりがな英和辞典

The companion to the essential dictionary for all students of Japanese.
• Furigana readings added to all *kanji* • 14,000-word basic vocabulary
Paperback, 728 pages; ISBN 4-7700-2751-6

KODANSHA'S ROMANIZED JAPANESE-ENGLISH DICTIONARY

新装版 ローマ字和英辞典

A portable reference written for beginning and intermediate students.
• 16,000-word basic vocabulary • No knowledge of *kanji* necessary
Paperback, 688 pages; ISBN 4-7700-2753-2

KODANSHA'S CONCISE ROMANIZED JAPANESE-ENGLISH DICTIONARY

コンサイス版 ローマ字和英辞典

A first, basic dictionary for beginner students of Japanese.
• 10,000-word basic vocabulary • Easy-to-find romanized entries listed in alphabetical order
• Definitions written for English-speaking users
• Sample sentences in romanized and standard Japanese script, followed by English translations
Paperback, 480 pages; ISBN 4-7700-2849-0

KODANSHA'S BASIC ENGLISH-JAPANESE DICTIONARY

日本語学習 基礎英日辞典

An annotated dictionary useful for both students and teachers.
• Over 4,500 headwords and 18,000 vocabulary items • Examples and information on stylistic differences
• Appendices for technical terms, syntax and grammar
Paperback , 1520 pages; ISBN 4-7700-2895-4

THE MODERN ENGLISH-NIHONGO DICTIONARY

日本語学習 英日辞典

The first truly bilingual dictionary designed exclusively for non-native learners of Japanese.
• Over 6,000 headwords • Both standard Japanese (with *furigana*) and romanized orthography
• Sample sentences provided for most entries • Numerous explanatory notes and *kanji* guides
Vinyl flexibinding, 1200 pages; ISBN 4-7700-2148-8

www.thejapanpage.com

KODANSHA INTERNATIONAL DICTIONARIES

Easy-to-use dictionaries designed for non-native learners of Japanese.

KODANSHA'S ELEMENTARY KANJI DICTIONARY

新装版 教育漢英熟語辞典

A first, basic *kanji* dictionary for non-native learners of Japanese.
• Complete guide to 1,006 *Shin-kyōiku kanji*   • Over 10,000 common compounds
• Three indices for finding *kanji*   • Compact, portable format   • Functional, up-to-date, timely
Paperback, 576 pages; ISBN 4-7700-2752-4

KODANSHA'S ESSENTIAL KANJI DICTIONARY

新装版 常用漢英熟語辞典

A functional character dictionary that is both compact and comprehensive.
• Complete guide to the 1,945 essential *jōyō kanji*   • 20,000 common compounds
• Three indices for finding *kanji*
Paperback , 928 pages; ISBN 4-7700-2891-1

THE KODANSHA KANJI LEARNER'S DICTIONARY

新装版 漢英学習字典

The perfect kanji tool for beginners to advanced learners.
• Revolutionary SKIP lookup method   • Five lookup methods and three indices
• 2,230 entries and 41,000 meanings for 31,000 words
Paperback, 1060 pages (2-color); ISBN 4-7700-2855-5

KODANSHA'S EFFECTIVE JAPANESE USAGE DICTIONARY

新装版 日本語使い分け辞典

A concise, bilingual dictionary which clarifies the usage of frequently confused words and phrases.
• Explanations of 708 synonymous terms   • Numerous example sentences
Paperback, 768 pages; ISBN 4-7700-2850-4

KODANSHA'S DICTIONARY OF BASIC JAPANESE IDIOMS

日本語イディオム辞典

All idioms are given in Japanese script and romanized text with English translations. There are
approximately 880 entries, many of which have several senses.
Paperback, 672 pages; ISBN 4-7700-2797-4

A DICTIONARY OF JAPANESE PARTICLES

てにをは辞典

Treats over 100 particles in alphabetical order, providing sample sentences for each meaning.
• Meets students' needs from beginning to advanced levels
• Treats principal particle meanings as well as variants
Paperback, 368 pages; ISBN 4-7700-2352-9

A DICTIONARY OF BASIC JAPANESE SENTENCE PATTERNS

日本語基本文型辞典

Author of the best-selling All About Particles explains fifty of the most common, basic patterns
and their variations, along with numerous contextual examples. Both a reference and a textbook
for students at all levels.
• Formulas delineating basic pattern structure   • Commentary on individual usages
Paperback, 320 pages; ISBN 4-7700-2608-0

The best-selling language course is now even better!

JAPANESE FOR BUSY PEOPLE Revised Edition

改訂版　コミュニケーションのための日本語　全3巻

Association for Japanese-Language Teaching (AJALT)

The leading textbook for conversational Japanese has been improved to make it easier than ever to teach and learn Japanese.

- Transition to advancing levels is more gradual.
- Kana version available for those who prefer Japanese script. Audio supplements compatible with both versions.
- English-Japanese glossary added to each volume.　• Short *kanji* lessons introduced in Volume II.
- Clearer explanations of grammar.　　　　　• Shorter, easy-to-memorize dialogues.

Volume I

Teaches the basics for communication and provides a foundation for further study.

- Additional appendices for grammar usage.

Text	paperback, 232 pages	ISBN 4-7700-1882-7
Text / Kana Version	paperback, 256 pages	ISBN 4-7700-1987-4
Cassette Tapes	three cassette tapes (total 120 min.)	ISBN 4-7700-1883-5
Compact Discs	two compact discs (total 120 min.)	ISBN 4-7700-1909-2
The Workbook	paperback, 192 pages	ISBN 4-7700-1907-6
The Workbook Cassette Tapes	two cassette tapes (total 100 min.)	ISBN 4-7700-1769-3
Japanese Teacher's Manual	paperback, 160 pages	ISBN 4-7700-1906-8
English Teacher's Manual	paperback, 244 pages	ISBN 4-7700-1888-6

Volume II

Provides the basic language skills necessary to function in a professional environment.

Text	paperback, 288 pages	ISBN 4-7700-1884-3
Text / Kana Version	paperback, 296 pages	ISBN 4-7700-2051-1
Compact Discs	three compact discs (total 200 min.)	ISBN 4-7700-2136-4
The Workbook	paperback, 260 pages	ISBN 4-7700-2037-6
The Workbook Cassette Tapes	three cassette tapes (total 130 min.)	ISBN 4-7700-2111-9
Japanese Teacher's Manual	paperback, 168 pages	ISBN 4-7700-2036-8

Volume III

Expands vocabulary and structure to bring the student to the intermediate level.

Text	paperback, 256 pages	ISBN 4-7700-1886-X
Text / Kana Version	paperback, 296 pages	ISBN 4-7700-2052-X
Compact Discs	three compact discs (total 200 min.)	ISBN 4-7700-2137-2
The Workbook	paperback, 288 pages	ISBN 4-7700-2331-6
The Workbook Cassette Tapes	two cassette tapes (total 100 min.)	ISBN 4-7700-2358-8
Japanese Teacher's Manual	paperback, 200 pages	ISBN 4-7700-2306-5

Kana Workbook

Straightforward text for quick mastery of *hiragana* and *katakana* utilizing parallel learning of reading, writing, listening and pronunciation.

- Grids for writing practice.　• Reading and writing exercises.
- Optional audio tape aids in pronunciation.

Text	paperback, 80 pages	ISBN 4-7700-2096-1
Cassette Tape	one cassette tape (40 min.)	ISBN 4-7700-2097-X

JAPANESE FOR PROFESSIONALS　ビジネスマンのための実戦日本語

Association for Japanese-Language Teaching (AJALT)

A serious and detailed manual of the language of trade, commerce, and government. Fourteen lessons introduce common business situations with key sentences and a dialogue to illustrate proper usage.

Paperback, 256 pages; ISBN 4-7700-2038-4